ACTIVATE LEADERSHIP

ACTIVATE LEADERSHIP

ASPEN TRUTHS
TO EMPOWER
MILLENNIAL LEADERS

JON MERTZ

"The most difficult thing is the decision to act. The rest is merely tenacity. The fears are paper tigers. You can do anything you decide to do. You can act to change and control your life; and the procedure, the process is its own reward."

— Amelia Earhart

*To the next generation of leaders who
lead on purpose.*

CONTENTS

ASPEN MANIFESTO

FOR MILLENNIAL LEADERS

1. LIKE ASPENS, YOU ARE DESIGNED TO THRIVE. LEAD WITH WHAT UNIQUELY STIRS YOUR HEART, MIND, AND SOUL.

2. YOU MOVE MORE QUICKLY THAN OTHER GENERATIONS. BE PATIENT, BUT DON'T WAIT FOR APPROVAL FROM OTHERS ON WHAT MATTERS MOST.

3. YOU CONNECT MORE WIDELY THAN ANY GENERATION. ACTIVATE THAT CONNECTION ADVANTAGE TO BUILD TRUE RELATIONSHIPS AND COLLABORATE TO CREATE.

4. DEMAND MEANINGFUL WORK AND IGNITE SPARKS FOR YOUR PEERS TO LEAD ON PURPOSE.

5. DON'T GET STUCK IN INFORMATION ANALYSIS. READILY CONVERT WHAT YOU LEARN INTO CONSTRUCTIVE ACTIONS AND REAL RESULTS.

FOREWORD

Perhaps you are a Millennial leader looking for your next revolutionary inspiration. Or, you are exploring ways to excel on your current life path. Whatever your reason is for reading this book, as a Millennial, I get it. It all boils down to the fact that we all want to change the world—for the better. But we can't do it overnight, and we can't do it alone. We need buy in from the other generations, or our efforts will forever be labeled as a frivolous fight.

For our generation to be legendary, another "Great Generation" of leaders, we need not only to be persuasive in our message, but we also must genuinely acknowledge the wisdom and experience that the generations before us have available. If we listen closely enough, we can hear their advice and insights. Our argument, at the core, has to be transparent, too, so that the ultimate value of our endeavors to humanity is obvious and not disguised by what could be perceived as temporarily selfish motives. I read a comment recently on LinkedIn in which a woman named Ardith McCann summed up this concept humbly: "If we claim intelligence, then we must accept the responsibility of being part of the continuum."

As a part of the continuum, Jon Mertz gets it, too. I have had the privilege to know Jon for over four years working with him and witnessing his leadership research firsthand. His book is written for us, intended to encourage us and spark our motivation to be that next great generation of leaders. The inspiring part is that he already believes we have the potential to become legendary, but he identifies gaps in our perspective and potential.

Activate Leadership lays out crucial concepts that are both provocative and inspiring. Jon recognizes our generation as the most connected socially and the most educated in a long line of history, and with those skills we do in fact have the power to change the world—for the better.

But drawing from surprising sources of wisdom, Jon helps us leverage our relationships. There are more people in the Baby Boomer generation than there are in our generation, so we have a plethora of potential mentors at

our fingertips. Activate Leadership offers a critical starting point for your journey as a leader.

When we activate leadership, as Jon suggests, we can make
a dynamic impact on future generations—for the better.

With you,
Erica Johansen

@TheGr8Chalupa

INTRODUCTION: BEYOND GOING IT ALONE

"IN EVERY WALK WITH NATURE ONE
RECEIVES FAR MORE THAN HE SEEKS."

- JOHN MUIR
NATURALIST, EXPLORER, WRITER,
AND CONSERVATIONIST

I had originally wanted to go it alone on my first snowshoe venture in the Colorado Rockies. Most of my days were spent managing a growing company as vice president of marketing for a healthcare corporation, and as an entrepreneur focused on leadership and career development through an online community called Thin Difference. I needed a break from the non-stop flow of work and meetings. I wanted to be alone to get perspective on a problem that had been bugging me.

In both my work as VP and as an entrepreneur I kept butting up against a leadership gap that seemed to be a generation gap: The twenty-somethings I worked with and studied online had seemingly different views about what it means to work and lead than what I and colleagues near my age seemed to hold. For the first time in several years, I felt challenged as a VP to manage my teams effectively and with integrity. As a father of two teenage boys, one in college and one in high school, I wondered if this difference was just another "generation gap" cliché, or was there something truly distinct about this generation of Millennials.

Older generations point at certain statistics and pigeonhole Millennials with tags like these:

- JOB-HOPPING: The average 25-year-old probably has already worked in 6.3 different jobs since being 18.[1]

- ME, ME, ME: From the cover of *Time* magazine to many subsequent articles, fingers point at Millennials as being self-centered and focused on instant gratification. In a Career Builder survey, 85% of hiring managers and human-resource executives

---

1   Annalyn Kurtz. "Job-hopping millennials no different than their parents." CNN, April 9, 2013.

feel they have a stronger sense of entitlement than older workers.[2]

- SOCIALLY BUT SUPERFICIALLY CONNECTED: 84 percent of Millennials are social media users and over 80% sleep with phones.[3] An "always on" generation wears on other generations.

Older leaders shrug their shoulders as they watch the world change. Millennials see older leaders as obstacles to creating the change they want to make. The challenge is two-fold: One, if older generations are closing the door on Millennials because of incomplete stereotypes, then how much will be lost in advancing our future on a solid common ground? A trust gap widens between generations. More notably, a leadership gap grows.

Two, you as Millennials do have to leverage your strengths if you are going to change the world for the better for the long term and not just the short term—thus, repeating the very mistakes of your forebears only in glitzier, more high-tech and speedier ways.

---

2   "The 'Trophy Kids' Go to Work." *Wall Street Journal*, October 21, 2008.

3   "How Digital Behavior Differs Among Millennials, Gen Xers and Boomers," *eMarketer*, March 21, 2013.

I was of two minds: On one hand, I could see Millennials' remarkable potential as leaders, and I wanted to embrace them and nurture their growth. On the other hand, they seemed to have such a radically different outlook and set of values that they seemed immune to any guidance I could give.

Being alone in the Rockies, I thought, might help me unwind and see the problem more clearly.

"You could die going out on your own," the young woman renting me the snowshoes said. Evidently, an avalanche had happened recently and some new snowshoers had perished in the wild.

So there I stood in my newly rented shoes, waiting among a group of strangers for a guide. Ethan and Cole, my two teenage sons, flew off skiing, and it was my first time snowshoeing in my forty-eight years.

Our group of ten trudged through the snow at different speeds, one couple shuttling ahead, others lagging behind; so the guide stopped us frequently to keep the group together. Impatient, I wondered if I should have heeded my original idea and launched off on my own. But my fear of being buried beneath an avalanche held me back.

The trees were thick and faceless as we marched on, each step an effort. While skiing seemed fast and easy, snow-shoeing was a workout. *Why on earth did I need these tennis rackets on my feet? Where was the peace and perspective I had traveled for?*

Then, our surroundings changed. We were thick in a grove of tall, lean, vibrant trees, diverse in size and age. Their silvery bark reflected the sun so the aspen shone like light against the snow. I felt my breath catch and my irritation—with my shoes and this slowpoke group—drain.

The guide stopped, and I remember a loud silence before she spoke. "You will never see an aspen alone."

She was right. I hadn't ever seen just a single aspen tree.

"They are always in a community," she said. "You see, aspens are bound together by their huge, incredible root systems."

I felt trivial. Small and unimportant within a thriving grove. I imagined their roots beneath my snowshoes, vast and connected.

The guide continued, "They collaborate through their root connections and work as a grove to sustain a healthy community."

It was odd, but I began to see similarities and feel a kindred spirit between aspens and Millennials. I saw my sons reflected in those trees. I saw the Millennial generation: connection-rich, purpose-filled, and community-centered.

I returned home equipped with a new perspective, a renewed project, and a new yet ancient source of wisdom to communicate with these younger leaders possessed with potential.

Activate Leadership: Aspen Truths to Empower Millennial Leaders was conceived.

THIN DIFFERENCE

I did not expect to be embraced by aspen trees that afternoon in the Rockies, but experience has taught me that sparks that inspire new direction in life and career can happen anywhere if you are open and choose to listen.

After returning home, I dug into learning as much as I could about aspens and what made them work. I compared those notes with my years of exploring youth leadership. I updated ways to develop students into thinking like a leader early on.

Thin Difference found a renewed direction. Thin Difference began as a way to express my thoughts about life and leadership. As my reflections refined and my audience grew, Thin Difference became more than just a blog; it became a community to encourage, challenge, and engage others in our leadership craft. As I read other sites, I saw more and more veteran leaders and business people finger-pointing at and stereotyping Millennials. Blaming seemed designed to score SEO points rather than foster each other's leadership skills.

Among the aspens, another transformation took hold. I decided to evolve Thin Difference into an intergenerational forum designed to support the next generation of leaders. Today, over half of my website traffic comes from Millennials and Generation Z (according to current Google Analytics). Also, Thin Difference has become a top site for leadership topics and exchanges. In looking at a recent leadership blog ranking, the Alexa ranking of Thin Difference puts it squarely in the top 20 sites.

Trust Across America-Trust Around the World then recognized Thin Difference as one of the <u>Top 100 Thought Leaders for Trustworthy Business</u>. Their reason:

> Having chosen to invest in building and strengthening the relationships across generations in the

workplace and beyond, Jon is an advocate and thought leader in helping Millennials discover their uniquely powerful expression as leaders so they can make the biggest possible contribution in the world.

I'm humbled. All of this in part by listening to those aspens. By working together and challenging each other, we can become better leaders, no matter our generation. I have found a surprising openness on both sides of the perceived leadership gap. Millennials and non-Millennials alike are eager to learn from each other. This is the mission of Thin Difference.

And I discovered what my real purpose is: guiding, championing, challenging, and inspiring Millennial leaders. I encourage inter-generational conversations to strengthen conscious leadership, build stronger teams, and lead a richer life.

It turns out there really is a thin difference in that perceived generation gap.

MILLENNIAL LEADERSHIP

I see how purpose-driven and well-educated you are, ready to adapt and grow. The only relevant statistic is this: In

2020, Millennials will make-up about fifty percent of the workforce (Meister, 2012).[4] With this presence, keen leadership is essential. You have many advantages born from technology and education advancements. Like aspens, your roots run deep and wide.

You Millennials can lead with a bigger story, create better solutions, and guide with greater meaning. The question is, *Will you get too distracted by the stereotypes and anxiousness to make a big difference as soon as possible? Will you rise to your potential and bring out the qualities uniquely suited to meet the challenges of the early twenty-first century?*

Will you, in other words, activate leadership?

ACTIVATE LEADERSHIP & LEAD ON PURPOSE

Your generation, more than any before you, understands that purpose is more than an ideal; it is a way of life and leadership. We have heard "purpose-driven" and "leading

---

4   The 2020 Workplace: How Innovative Companies Attract, Develop, and Keep Tomorrow's Employees Today, Jeanne C. Meister and Karie Willyerd, May 11, 2010.

in purpose" many times before. *Leading on purpose* combines these two ideas:

- You are intentional, aware, and growing in how you lead.

- Whether it's the initiative itself or the interactions you facilitate, there is an endearing purpose to the work undertaken, the relationships developed, and the ideas pursued.

This book draws fresh, dynamic leadership skills from the ancient wisdom of thriving aspen groves to help you hone your skills and traits to lead effectively and on purpose.

To lead on purpose, there are four key principles gleaned from the wisdom of aspens, Aspen Truths. Each of the four core chapters defines one Aspen Truth and lays out skillful strategies that will help you activate your innate Millennial traits into leadership strengths.

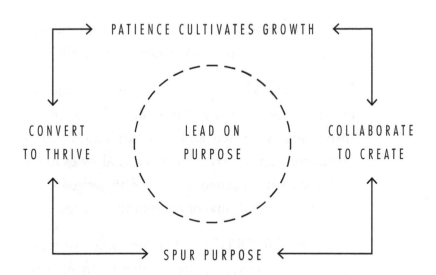

- **PATIENCE CULTIVATES GROWTH:** Being patient is often erected as a barrier between two generations—a generational difference of giving and wanting opportunity. In reality, a tempo exists between doing the required work and stepping up to the next level of performance and impact. This is the true nature of patience, and we will discover ways to get this relationship and timing right.

- **COLLABORATE TO CREATE:** Connecting is easy, especially in a social world. To make a real, lasting difference, connections help but they are dormant unless used to engage and collaborate. Understanding where your connections stand will facilitate a more productive, meaningful, and collaborative approach to create more and produce real results.

- SPUR PURPOSE: Purpose is discussed frequently, and much too often it remains talk or just a feeling. Inspiration is needed and so is aspiration. Combined, you can inspire others and lead by example in doing what is needed to achieve bigger goals and a higher organizational or community purpose.

- CONVERT TO THRIVE: At a time when so much information is available along with ways to learn extensively about ourselves, there is a danger in being buried to a point of inaction. The number one skill to excel is the ability to convert. Learning all you can about your market, industry, field, and yourself will exponentially, positively enhance your leadership-ability when you take the next step to convert ideas and knowledge into tangible results.

With well over eighty million Millennials entering the workplace, soon you will be the dominant generation, standing among declining older generations. You will lead the next generation on purpose. You feel you are born to lead, and you probably are. But you don't have to take it from me. To activate your innate leadership potential, tap into an ancient source of wisdom. Aspen truths.

ASPEN TRUTH 1
PATIENCE CULTIVATES GROWTH

LEADING IS ABOUT TEMPO.

FIND YOUR PACE AND TIME YOUR STRIDE.

When Ben Simon and Mia Zavalij ate at the dining hall where they were students at the University of Maryland, College Park, they noticed something that bugged them: Good, untouched, and potential "leftovers" were being thrown out. Just around the immediate area, Ben and Mia knew first-hand how many people went hungry.

Whereas many people might have noticed the same problem, Ben and Mia had an idea. What if leftovers from all college campuses could feed the hungry in their local area? Through partnerships with other colleges and universities, soon the <u>Food Recovery Network</u> became a reality. In less than two years, the Food Recovery Network achieved full non-profit status and continues to add new national chapters regularly, serving over 135,000 meals to needy people in various cities around the United States.

Innovative? Yes. Impatient? Yes. Effective? Yes. Such speed to act is a trait I see in Millennials.

INNOVATIVE, IMPATIENT MILLENNIALS

Your generation leans toward innovation and creative boldness. Two-thirds of Millennials surveyed say innovation is a key ingredient in selecting a place to work. Once at work, sixty percent think employers are innovative. Half of Millennials believe the organization they work for supports innovation while an equal amount think it would be easier to innovate if self-employed.[5]

---

5   The Millennial Survey 2014, Deloitte, January 2014.

Along with an innovative mindset, you are eager. You want to execute, share, and launch those ideas, now. You're ready to make your big difference in the world. The idea of waiting, of putting in 10,000 hours of deliberate practices, seems antiquated and unnecessary.

But here's the problem you face: Couple constant innovation with hyper-connectedness, and impatience rises exponentially. You have instant access to resources once restricted to a few: information and people. In February 2012, a Pew Research study entitled "Millennials Will Benefit and Suffer Due to Their Hyperconnected Lives"[6] suggested you may be wired differently—more nimble in day-to-day activities, but more impatient in longer-term initiatives. The adaptive, networked style "...will drive [Millennials] to thirst for instant gratification, settle for quick choices, and lack patience."

Patience is the problem. But it is not the problem in the way you would expect.

My work with multiple generations and my assessment of what makes Millennials potentially unique leaders reveals

---

6   "Millennials will benefit and suffer due to their hyper-connected lives," Pew Research Internet Project, Janna Anderson and Lee Rainie, February 29, 2012.

that the answer to this dilemma, oddly enough, has something to do with *not* being patient. By "patience" I don't mean some paternal adage of "Wait your turn" or "Wait until you've paid your dues." Patience is different than waiting or biding your time. Waiting is sitting on the sidelines, not doing the work.

Patient leaders don't wait. They want. They yearn to achieve something bigger and better. Patient leaders are passionate, but they know how to pace their passion.

- How do you leverage your desire to make a difference sooner than later?

- How can you lead in a way that will sustain you — not for the next few months or years — but for the next few decades?

- How do you partner with patience while keeping stride with your passion?

What is surprising is that there are times for growth spurts. There are times and opportunities for impatience. Your challenge is to activate your advantages for long-term and sustainable leadership—not just short-term gain.

Again, don't take my word for it.

ASPEN TRUTH #1

Aspens are survivors and thrivers thanks to an ancient system. Aspen roots can remain dormant for thousands of years, yet at the right time they jump to life and regenerate as a community. Under the surface, there is a massive root system supporting many younger saplings that will grow in strength. Older trees will die. However, with a well-built root system, the foundation can survive for thousands of years, supporting growth, new growth, and an ongoing presence.

When disturbances happen, aspens weather the change. Even when all above ground is wiped out by fire or mudslides, aspens spring to life from their roots when all is clear above.

Aspens have a fundamental approach to surviving and thriving over the long-term. Patience Cultivates Growth—that is Aspen Truth #1.

ASPEN TRUTH #1: Patience Cultivates Growth. Patience is not about waiting your turn. Patience sets a pace to learning and strengthening your capabilities by doing the work. But know when to pump your pace to a stride to achieve your career goals and personal passions.

For Millennials, the Activate Leadership approach is simple: Be patient for growth. Discern the value of patience at the right times as well as the value of a speedier pace to grow your business or career at the right times. There are two essential branches of Aspen Truth #1 to consider.

1. KNOW YOUR FLOW BETWEEN HEART AND MIND.

Having passion in your career is vital as it feeds your mindset in how you solve problems, work with others, and achieve results. When passion turns to impatience or just an attitude of "doing it my way," it leads to career-hopping or disgruntled team relationships.

Passion alone is an incomplete answer. Passion requires pairing your heart and mind. To cultivate the fire within takes work and time to hone your skills and learn from others. Call it intelligent passion. There is a real business and career truth within this approach.

Aspens know it. Tending to their roots and sharing between young and old creates a foundation in which their passion shows its full color. There is a time to prepare and a time to spring.

Pacing—the art and science of timing—is a skill to learn and master. Discerning the timing to reach higher—stride—involves a mix of individual readiness, aligned heart and mind flow, and maybe a community nudge at times.

2. TEND YOUR ROOTS OF TRUST.

Challenges in life and work inevitably will throw you off-center. A series of innovative victories and praise can swell your ego and lead you into self-delusion. A series of creative failures and hardships can deflate your confidence. Like aspen roots, your foundation needs vital nutrients to sustain you in good times and bad. Your foundational nutrients, regardless of circumstances, are your beliefs.

Know the answers to these two key questions:

- What beliefs will keep you centered when times are really good?

- What beliefs will keep you motivated when times are really bad?

Reflection produces change and better results. What we do with each creates an advantage in how we lead. A balanced partnership between wise patience and impassioned impatience creates a better path forward.

Let's unpack each of these branches to help you activate your innate leadership potential.

ACTIVATE LEADERSHIP

1. KNOW YOUR FLOW BETWEEN HEART AND MIND.

You can grow frustrated thinking you must wait a lifetime to achieve your deepest goals. But when the right partnering happens between patience and impatience, a certain persistence takes hold. You become a leader with tempo.

To become a leader with tempo, first learn to discern. Be able to quickly discern daily activities, tasks, and decisions into one of two categories: inconsequential or consequential. This discernment is a skill and becomes near-instinctual for some leaders, but for others it requires dedicated practice. So, let's break it down.

Something **inconsequential** may seem important in the immediate moment but not in the long term. Most inconsequential things are forgotten a year later, and no one remembers what they were, or why they were important in the moment. **Consequential** actions and decisions create sustaining change for an organization. They are tied to an organization's vision, goals, and strategies to effect real growth.

It turns out that some inconsequential activities require patience and some impatience. Some consequential activities also require patience whereas other require impatience. So, with awareness and practice, you can quickly discern which **inconsequential** activities require **patience** and which require **impatience** as well as which **consequential** activities require **patience** and which require **impatience**.

All this may seem complex, but in getting our tempo right we always need to determine when and how to make the smoothest moves. The following two-by-two matrix "A Leader's Tempo" can clarify how to think through this process. A few points:

- YOUR TEMPERAMENT: The left side—patience and impatience—describe how you may feel about what you are doing and how you may approach what needs to be done. Think of your temperament as what your heart is urging and cautioning.

- YOUR ACTIVITY TYPES: When considering the type of activities, they can be classified as either having consequence or not.

- YOUR STRATEGY: When matching your temperament with the activity type, a relevant strategy is suggested on how to act and move forward. This is where your mind is engaged to lead in a thoughtful, growth-oriented way.

Leadership is a combination of how you view challenges, classify choices, and then act. With this clarification, let's walk through finding your leadership tempo.

A LEADER'S TEMPO

PATIENT	ROUTINE	STRIDE
IMPATIENT	RELEASE	PACE
	INCONSEQUENTIAL	CONSEQUENTIAL

ROUTINE: There are inconsequential tasks, activities we must do, obligations we must fulfill in order to execute otherwise meaningful projects and missions. Leaders learn to make certain inconsequential tasks, which require patience, a routine. They are logistical details or other tasks not overtly tied to our big dreams and bold goals. In leadership, the routine elements can be managing quarterly and annual performance reviews, participating in meetings to review project milestones, and developing budgets to keep finances in line.

Routines test the patience of many visionary, innovative Millennials who like to focus on the big picture but not the detailed routines, yet routines are necessary for a team or business to grow productively over the long-term. If you lean toward the visionary, it's best if you can partner with or team with detail-oriented people who are patient with inconsequential routine.

Fulfill routine responsibilities, but don't let routines dominate your time and attention. If you invest most of your time and energy in daily routines, you risk slipping into mediocrity. Similarly, if you tend to get stuck in details, try to partner or team with people who help you keep the big picture intact.

RELEASE: If you get impatient frequently with inconsequential activities, you risk getting worn out. In leading, you will find team dynamics and individual personalities that interrupt progress, see meetings mismanaged, and experience time wasted. These are unpredictable, inconsequential activities—very different from the routines necessary to keep an organization growing sustainably. Avoid investing lots of emotion in these inconsequential disruptions.

Instead, release tension and stay focused on solutions. Release is a skill you can learn and apply. When someone gets under your skin, rather than react with anger, release the feeling and respond with a question or statement that steers the conversation back to the objective at hand. Learn to let go of what seems to matter in the moment but matters little in the long haul.

PACE: Some **consequential** activities rile us up. Challenges arise. If we don't focus on the right things, we stall progress and growth. In some cases, consequential activities require speed and impatience.

In a large-scale pricing and configuration project, I became the newly minted project manager. The project was a huge overhaul of enterprise applications and business processes, from supply chain to customer interactions. Key processes were being discussed and technical architectures being drawn up, but we were moving in very slow motion. We were getting muddled in meetings rather than completing activities. I was restless about what needed to be accomplished, as was the client. We needed to have new processes defined and approved. We needed technical specifications done so development work could begin. We needed to be prototyping the new approach and solution.

It would have been easy to host even more meetings and create a mirage of activity. Instead, I went back to the basics: we realigned project plans, gathered users to develop real specifications, and did the necessary work, one step at a time. We delivered the prototype on schedule, a tangible milestone delivered.

When you need to lead with impatience in consequential work, concentrate on setting a solid, meaningful pace. Doing so helps team members and employees feel confident in being able to accomplish a set of tasks or a project both on time and well.

STRIDE: The flip side of keeping pace is knowing when to stride. A stride is a long step; it's achieving the big missions, the initiatives that no one expected to happen. When you take the opportunity to lead with stride during consequential activities, you can shift your career and take rise to a new leadership level.

In my late twenties, I worked in Washington, DC. I had a decent job, a good salary, but I could feel my life and career stagnating. I longed to develop my leadership potential. I quit my job to pursue my MBA in Austin, Texas. Going from a good job to being a full-time student felt like both a big step up and a step back. I was paying money instead of making money. I was taking two years out of my career track to study. But a stride is a patient investment. Having no job at all was a big change and challenging, but without taking this stride my leadership development would have been sidetracked.

What would have happened if I hadn't taken the stride? One of two things would have happened. I would have been laid off during the administration change that happened two years later, and I would have been unemployed with many other political appointees. Or, I would have become a career government employee. In both cases, I would have taken a step back in realizing my work potential, and any big career ideas I had would have disappeared completely.

Aligning patience with consequential activities produces a wake-up call. Don't be so patient in developing your leadership capabilities that opportunities pass you by. Consider where you are and what your main leadership and purpose-filled goals are. Is the stage set for your next level of performance? Discern when the time is right to push yourself to take bigger steps, and then move forward and upward. Pump up your stride.

The challenge of pace and stride is to know when. No stock formula exists to apply, but the "A Leader's Tempo" matrix provides a way to think through your career, business, and leadership opportunities and roadblocks. Given this, consider how your heart and mind match up with stride and pace. Your heart will ache with wanting to do more, and your mind will raise its guard against taking the risks. Neither is wrong. In the middle of the flow lies the decision to make.

Let's put it this way:

1. TAKE THE STRIDE if your heart and mind are telling you the same thing. In other words, there is an intelligent passion to taking the step up. This doesn't mean you need to know everything, but you need to know enough to navigate the new growth paths ahead.

2. AVOID TAKING THE STRIDE if your heart and mind are in conflict and you churn to find the right answer. Understand what is fueling the uncertainty. Write those elements down and then patiently do the work to eliminate them.

3. KEEP THE PACE if your heart is at ease yet your mind is yearning to learn more. Dig in and expand your skills and capabilities. Keep the discipline of learning and doing the necessary work. If you have a career direction set, then understand what types of capabilities successful leaders have in this position today and enhance yours. Keep your pace in learning and growing.

4. DISRUPT YOUR PACE if you are losing enthusiasm for what you are doing. Disrupt your pace if you are not learning anything new. Look back over the past year, and ask yourself if you have learned a new skill, strengthened a key leadership trait, or engaged in a new initiative. If not, time may be calling to your heart and mind to re-engage and step-up.

Understanding your pace and stride relates to listening to your heart and mind. Some leaders meditate to explore this flow. Some leaders unplug completely to discern what the next steps should be. Others may just take a vacation and get away to think with greater clarity of what to do next.

Leading with soul is knowing your flow and tapping into it. Although no one can know you as well as you do, use your community to test your assumptions and direction. Use your community to hold you accountable and challenge you.

Overall, consider these axioms:

A LEADER'S TEMPO

	INCONSEQUENTIAL	CONSEQUENTIAL
PATIENT	ROUTINE	STRIDE
IMPATIENT	RELEASE	PACE

ROUTINE solves minor activities and issues.

RELEASE moves you beyond what doesn't matter.

ROUTINE and RELEASE keep you balanced in easy and tough times.

PACE keeps you centered when you need to move quickly.

STRIDE motivates you when you need to endure a set of long-term tasks or a long-term but high-stakes project.

PACE and STRIDE assure you're partnering patience and passion.

Keeping pace checks impatience. Leveraging stride checks patience. This balance supports natural leadership composure and self-assurance.

In determining when to pace and stride, use this guide and also consider the Leader's Tempo Self-Test.

Test where you are; then, realign your efforts.

A LEADER'S TEMPO

PATIENT	Am I being sucked in to just doing the same thing each and every day? Am I making progress forward on the BIG goals? **Get unstuck from your routines.**	Am I being sucked in to just doing the same thing each and every day? Am I making progress forward on the BIG goals? **Get unstuck from your routines.**
IMPATIENT	Am I being sucked in to just doing the same thing each and every day? Am I making progress forward on the BIG goals? **Get unstuck from your routines.**	Am I being sucked in to just doing the same thing each and every day? Am I making progress forward on the BIG goals? **Get unstuck from your routines.**
	INCONSEQUENTIAL	CONSEQUENTIAL

2. TEND TO YOUR LEADERSHIP ROOTS.

Leadership roots are simply what will support and deliver growth in your career and leadership. Roots create a foundation, and knowing what you believe and how you act from those beliefs form your leadership roots. Roots also absorb and distribute. Take a career cue—embrace knowledge from different sources and trust yourself to share, receive, and learn from success and failure. These are the essential elements of your leadership roots.

KNOW YOUR CORE BELIEFS

Your core beliefs are like nutrients to aspens; they keep you centered in good times and motivated in bad. When people challenge you, core beliefs root you. When situations try to deter or distract you, embracing your core beliefs connects you with the strong voice inside, your guide to navigate challenges. To grow your career and your business over the long-term, you have to know what you believe in and what you are willing to stand up for and lead by.

Define your core beliefs: How do you want to be known within your organization and community? When team members describe you, what words would you like them to use? Do your actions match the words you just imagined? If so, your core beliefs line up with your actions. When beliefs and actions align, that's integrity. Without firm core beliefs, we become flimsy as a leaf. Never be a flimsy leader. Lead with strong, evident core beliefs. Your beliefs will nourish you in your leadership growth.

ADMIT MISTAKES

Admitting mistakes results in making changes, engaging in challenging conversations, asking people to leave, guiding people into self-improvement, coaching others to find their purpose in work, and standing up for what is right and against what is wrong.

Admitting when a team member isn't right for a position is a tough call. I had a team member who was earnest and genuine. Although he had reasonable skills, he wasn't grasping our complex product. His performance wasn't meeting the timing or quality standards we had and being late and incomplete was adversely impacting other team members. I had to let him go.

Admitting when something isn't working is tough yet necessary for all involved. In my situation, I hired a high-value addition to my team, and the person I let go went on to work for a company that better fit his career desires. Making tough decisions sets the stage for better outcomes.

Without making these tough decisions, leadership roots weaken. Team members who are not living up to the organizational purpose or team requirements will wear on you and other team members. Leaving the wrong person in the wrong role will send the signal that weeds are okay and will be tolerated.

A big inconsistency between your leadership principles and actions will weaken your roots and the people who depend upon you. Make the right decision in the right way, learn from your mistakes, and everyone involved will learn and strengthen themselves in new ways.

TRUST TENSION

When impatient with a project's execution, the business's growth, or your own advancement, it's easy to be resentful of any kind of tension, obstacles, or mistake. The well-paced leader, however, learns how to trust tension and *use* tension to determine if it is time to take a bigger stride.

Tension means, in part, that which stretches us. The word comes from the same root as tendon and has its origins in *to stretch*. Tension is inevitable when relating to other people or when goals are not advancing. The impatient leader might try one of two extremes—avoid tension altogether or blast through tension with near-tyrannical and impetuous demands. Neither leads to sustained growth for you, the leader, or the organization.

Embrace tension. Trust yourself. When you feel tension, ask, *Have I set the right pace and picked up my stride at the right times?*

TRUST YOURSELF IN THE FEEDBACK PROCESS

Any leader who is going to grow her own leadership potential or grow her organization must solicit right feedback from the right people. Anytime you ask for feedback, you become vulnerable. In vulnerable moments, you feel tension between feelings of acceptance and rejection. The reality is tension is an enlightening force; it tightens your ideas while heightening your awareness. Embracing productive tension through soliciting and receiving helpful feedback can result in improved thoughts, better concepts, and enhanced innovation.

Trust yourself. Be confident in what you think, try, and do. Self-trust is rooted in opportunity for personal growth.

Several years ago, I put my heart and soul into developing a new program for teen leaders. Putting the idea and concept out there was fun, but getting feedback on what others would do differently was challenging. One of my most dispiriting moments was when someone told me, "It just isn't unique enough." Being run-of-the-mill isn't what I was trying to produce, and it cut to my core. However, without that tense moment and honest feedback, I wouldn't have improved it, and it would have failed eventually.

TRUST OTHERS IN THE FEEDBACK PROCESS

If you're on a team, you inevitably experience tension. If you supervise others within an organization, you come face-to-face with your impatience with other people. Sometimes, what you perceive as their ineptitude stems from their lack of sufficient training or communication.

President Ronald Reagan popularized a phrase, "Trust but verify." In leading teams, the more appropriate statement may be, "Trust but hold accountable." Each individual is unique in his or her talents and gifts. To engage each other's talents, we need to trust one another. Two people will likely solve the same problem in two different ways. Is one way better than another? Maybe, but unless you let them solve the problem, they will never apply their learning to solving the next problem.

Being impatient is easy for a leader. "Just let me do that," we think. "I can do it faster by myself." A key question: Do you only want to be the leader of yourself? Although self-leadership is vital, real leaders embrace and engage real people.

Movements only happen when many join in. Initiatives only conclude successfully when the talents of many are tapped.

Trusting others is a key leadership principle. If you want the people on your team to grow, then explore and discover what they need to prosper in their work. Once individuals knows their role and has the needed tools, give them space, autonomy, support, and time.

ROOTED IN INNOVATION

Aspens know how to survive well in troubled and good times. They build a system to feed themselves and keep growing. When the main lateral root is severed, younger roots take on a renewed energy for growth. Similarly, when overcrowding is cleared by natural or unnatural acts, roots now have a clear view to grow and make their presence known. Aspens create a system of preparation, survival, and fostering future growth.

Your passion drives you and keeps you advancing. But impatience mixed with passion can combust. Your fervor and enthusiasm for a project or mission can burn out quickly, earning you a reputation for being fickle instead of innovative. Cultivate a patient passion by doing the work, honing the skills you need, and learning from young and old. An intelligent passion creates your system for sustainable purpose, career growth, leadership excellence, and continued innovation.

As a Millennial leader, finding your tempo requires that you look beyond just the immediate moment and lead on purpose. Learn the aspen way to build, grow, and spread your innovation and purpose wherever you are and plan to go.

In this way, you start to activate your innate leadership potential.

ASPEN ACTIONS

In your leadership practices, engage the following Aspen Actions:

- Know your core beliefs. Write them down. Memorize them so you can repeat them in trying times.

- Identify practices to understand and tap into your flow between heart and mind. Practices could include meditation, daily walks, running, or whatever gives you the opportunity to connect within. Understand your trigger and caution points.

- Unplug from the daily flotsam in regular intervals and discern where your time is spent being impatient and patient. Develop personal checkpoints to ensure momentum versus busy motion.

- Trust yourself and your conviction. Contribute always; never hold back. Find ways and places to share your knowledge, insights, and skills.

ASPEN TRUTH 2
CONNECT TO EXPAND.
COLLABORATE TO CREATE.

EFFECTIVE COLLABORATION REQUIRES
HIGH ENGAGEMENT AND TRUST.

Ooshma Garg appears well-connected. She is an accomplished entrepreneur. After her first venture Anapata was sold to LawWerx, she embarked on a second venture and is now the Founder of Gobble for which she attracted a well-known investor, LinkedIn co-founder Reid Hoffman. By age 24, she started two successful businesses, focused now on getting healthy meals to as many homes as possible.

You'd assume Garg's entrepreneurial success stems from her network of connections with investors, right?

Maybe, but maybe there's more to Garg's success story. The truth is usually more complicated. Garg reached out to individual investors with curiosity about their ideas and insights. She engaged them in conversations. She established relationships. Once connected, she shifted to collaboration—learning, interacting, and refining her eventual approach to any new business, and, in her case, gained valuable investors.

Connections are easy to make. Collaboration takes effort. Millennial leaders have an innate instinct to connect. Those new leaders who activate that connection instinct into a collaboration strength will be more likely to realize their dreams and strategies.

HOW DEEP DO YOUR CONNECTIONS GO?

Millennials are personally expressive. At least three-quarters of Millennials have created at least one social profile. One-in-five of you have posted a video of yourself online, and over half of you have posted a "selfie" (PewResearch

Center, 2014).[7] In a Cisco survey of almost 3,000 eighteen-to thirty-year-olds in fourteen different countries, more than fifty percent said the Internet was "an integral part of their lives—one as important as food, water, and even air—that they could not live without."[8]

That personal expressiveness disrupts the staid corporate culture of the past.

The question is, *How deep do your connections go?* It's one thing to reach out to and "like" or socially network with other veteran leaders and investors in various fields. It's a whole other enterprise to collaborate.

To advance your business or team in the 21st century and to make the real difference you yearn to effect, discern how to connect and how to collaborate. The potential is within you. The tools are within your reach.

This is your challenge and opportunity.

---

7   Paul Taylor, "More than half of Millennials have shared a 'selfie'," PewResearchCenter, March 4, 2014.

8   Graeme McMillan, "Study: 18- to 30-Year-Olds Say Internet as Important as Food, Water and Air," September 21, 2011.

- How do you know how deeply to engage in and commit to various initiatives or causes?

- When do you move from making connection into forging collaboration?

- In this era of connected communities, how does transparency enhance leadership and collaboration?

ASPEN TRUTH #2

The largest known aspen root system is in Utah, covers 106 acres, and weighs over 6,000 tons. That's the size of over eighty football fields and the weight of over 6,000 Ford Fiestas.

Connections create a foundation. Big foundation can mean big support whether from a team or from investors. Running an impressive network smoothly, though, takes coordinated flow and a well-orchestrated system.

Aspen roots do much more than connect. They also distribute nutrients to those who need it. Aspens have a shared root system, spawning "clones" to support new growth and sustain longevity. The roots support an interactive, problem-solving relationship. In other words, aspens collaborate through their connections. With the Activate Leadership approach, you can, too.

ASPEN TRUTH #2: Connect to Expand. Collaborate to Create. Draw from your innate expressiveness to connect with other people. When you do so wisely and authentically, you can expand your business network. But know when and how to shift from connection to collaboration in order to realize your entrepreneurial visions and initiatives.

You can collaborate with conviction of purpose to produce real results.

These three branches of Aspen Truth #2 can help you create a strong leadership foundation:

1. KNOW WHEN TO BE A CHAMPION.

You cannot expend your greatest enthusiasm for every endeavor and cause or else you will burn out and exhaust your potential. As a Millennial Leader, you can garner a few tools to help you quickly decide which projects merit your greatest zeal. When you know when and how to be a champion for a cause, you will inspire other team members and potential investors to support you.

2. PROGRESS ON PURPOSE.

Progress is not linear; detours happen. However, when you and your team make consistent accomplishments, you will see your line of progress. When you put the cause ahead of your career, you convey to your team or collaborators what your collective purpose is, and you will be more likely to build a resilient team. A resilient team that acts on purpose will be more likely to stay on-track while also better responding to likely challenges and unwanted surprises.

3. BE TRANSPARENT TO ASSURE FLOW.

When you clearly convey to someone else your goals and intentions, you go beyond connection-making. You're "letting someone in." You're building mutual trust. You're forging collaboration. In the case of aspens, nutrients flow seamlessly through underlying connections to points where needed. No second-guessing. No politics. Flow happens.

When flow happens in your endeavors, you and your collaborators can quickly identify where the trouble spots are, who needs help, and what assistance is needed to sustain flow.

You determine where to place your energy and when to use your connections to collaborate. When you do so, you activate your innate leadership potential. You rise to challenges, solve tough problems, and realize a new vision.

Let's unpack each of these frameworks to help you activate your innate leadership potential.

ACTIVATE LEADERSHIP

1. BE A CHAMPION.

Collaboration requires you to engage real people in real situations solving real problems. Engagement involves how you recognize and work with other people. Engagement also involves how deeply you choose to get involved in certain issues, projects, and causes.

WHAT'S YOUR ENGAGEMENT LEVEL?

Engagement is an attitude that expresses your degree of enthusiasm for a particular project or endeavor. You express your engagement through the amount of time and energy you expend on a cause, what you express verbally to others, and the actions you visibly take.

In my experience and studies, I have defined five levels of engagement. Not every project requires the same level of your and your colleagues' or team members' engagement. Become aware of these five levels to help you decide quickly which projects and causes merit your being their champion:

LEVEL 1 — IGNORANT: No awareness of people or issue

LEVEL 2 — FAMILIAR: Passing knowledge of person or issue

LEVEL 3 — COMPREHENSIVE: Base knowledge of person or issue

LEVEL 4 — INTERACTIVE: Conversational and on-topic; mutual interest leads to involvement in supporting a resolution to the issue or situation

LEVEL 5 — CHAMPION: Deeply engaged with others in solving issue, resolving a situation, or pursuing a cause; close identification with issue, situation, or cause

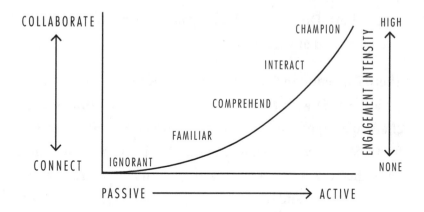

As the scale moves from Level 1 to Level 5, we move from a stationary state to an active one. It's the difference between describing a situation and acting upon one. When you move to a Level-5 action, your engagement intensity increases along with your collaborative approach. Level 5 means you care deeply about what is happening or what needs to happen.

A Level-5 engagement becomes part of your personal brand identity. You align so closely to the issue or cause that it becomes a part of who you are as a leader. Your engagement is intertwined with how you want to be identified as well as who you are identifying with.

To be a successful leader, know what you stand for, and match your engagement level to it. Remember, know your core beliefs. Doing so will help you discern when and how to engage and at what level.

There isn't enough time in a day or week to identify closely (at a Level 5) with all relevant causes, issues, problems, or challenges. Ignorance is not an option either. Here's what I mean: With my background in politics, I became concerned with the recent stalemates and inability of politicians to come together and solve our big financial challenges. My interest hovered around Level 3. However, when my research led me to an organization called No Labels, whose initiative aligned well with my interests and focus on future generations, I began to move up the engagement scale. No Labels is focused on eliminating the divisiveness in politics and shifting the focus to real problem-solving and consensus building. I eventually engaged at a Champion Level and hosted several local No Labels meetings in my community to raise awareness and get others involved. I collaborated with the organization by building new connections. I collaborated locally with my personal connections by getting others engaged to gain momentum around a cause.

Take the time to determine your right engagement level by being curious. Ask questions about situations, projects, and initiatives to test your interest, knowledge, and possible engagement.

Your leadership capability and direction will be more centered and activated in the right places at the right time when your core beliefs and purpose align.

Here's the moment of truth. To really get the pop in mutual efforts, your collaborative team needs to be at a similar level of engagement. If one person is at the Champion level and another person is at the Familiar, then your most important projects might flounder. If two out of five team members are two or three levels below Champion, then what will the overall effectiveness be? If five out of five team members are at the Champion engagement level, how much more can be accomplished?

If you are engaged at Level-4 Interactive or Level-5 Champion, how do you get others on your team to become Champions too for the right projects?

The answer: Transparency in the Collaborative Mix.

2. COLLABORATE WITH TRANSPARENCY.

Expressive Millennials are ripe to give Old School Collaboration a fresh approach as they tear down walls of secrecy and compartmentalization. Take David Karp, founder and CEO of Tumblr, purchased by Yahoo. David, a Millennial leader, builds a culture of freedom, responsibility, and opportunity to create and collaborate. David created work space for individual team members to solve customer problems, develop new features, and collaborate with each other. Time wasn't structured for predetermined meetings and long test cycles. They met to solve problems when needed. As a team, they generated ideas of what to develop next and listened closely to the customer community. When it came to testing new feature releases, it was "all hands on deck." Tumblr weaves a clear, collaborative environment. More importantly, it extends into the customer community. Connections turn into collaborative points of action and results.

Tumblr's actions reflect an international movement. Leaders around the globe have brought down workplace walls and replaced separate offices with diner style seating, tables, and white board walls. Gathering pods are set up for teams and co-workers to spontaneously and casually gather, leave project notes, and keep the daily project flow going -without the need for constant formal meetings. Collaboration, in other words, is becoming part of the Millennial workplace culture and habitat.

But here's the deal: White boards and dining style gathering places alone will not facilitate sustainable collaboration for high-engagement projects and causes. Those are only tools. It's up to human, emotional, intelligent leaders to facilitate true, long-lasting collaboration.

How do you lead a team to collaborate optimally on high-engagement projects?

WHEN DO YOU COLLABORATIVELY ENGAGE?

I have found that leaders need frameworks to help them make on-the-spot decisions and long-term strategies. The Collaborative Mix is a framework to help you weigh which projects require you to create a team of Champions.

CONNECT to raise awareness.

COLLABORATE to identify yourself and your partners, team members, or investors with a mission, issue, challenge, or cause, and work to resolve or change it.

THE COLLABORATIVE MIX

	LOW COLLABORATION HIGH	
HIGH	MUTUALLY INDEPENDENT	COLLABORATIVELY ENGAGED
CONNECTIONS		
LOW	AUTONOMOUS	PARTNER

Each quadrant highlights a collaborative approach given how an individual is connected and how they engage those connections. Let's explore each quadrant to determine when to leverage your connections to create, implement, and gain momentum.

AUTONOMOUS: When both the number of connections and the level of collaboration are low, a person acts essentially alone. It's a solo venture. The resources and the ability to achieve necessary results are within reach of the individual. You can achieve goals in this mode, but that achievement may not happen as broadly or as quickly. Working alone is, in general, less effective than a well-working team unless you need time to think.

Examples do not include individual tasks that are part of a collaborative project.

Examples do include your designing and programming your own website or blog. If you write, edit, design, and publish a book from start to finish on your own, that's also an autonomous project (good luck!). If you think through a concept or develop an individual experiment, those are autonomous efforts.

Key questions for you and your team members:

- Do you have enough connections to create effectively and achieve real results?

- How could greater collaboration raise the quality of your work and outcomes?

- How can you get others engaged in your initiative?

There are times when working alone may make sense as connections may just clutter thoughts or interrupt work. Consider the type of work required and which, if any, connections may assist you or your team in a productive way.

MUTUALLY INDEPENDENT: At this level, we connect a lot but collaborate little. This approach is a bit like a relay race. Each team member or participant does her or his part and hands off the baton or works simultaneously. Each individual performs his or her respective work and does it well. There is some interaction but no close collaboration. Independent, handoffs can be an effective way to get work done, but it may take more time and effort than some other approaches.

Many bureaucratic activities—such as the people involved in processing your taxes, your insurance claims, your driver's license—involve mutually independent activities. Some team projects such as website development, brand development, and book development operate at this level. A book manuscript can go from author to a series of editors to designers to promoters.

Here are key questions for you and your team members:

- How can greater collaboration enhance the efficiency of your activities within a process?

- Do you have enough leverage with your connections to accelerate your desired results?

- How can your raise the engagement levels of your connections?

If the work is strictly process-oriented and each "link" needs to play her or his role well, then focus to do your part. Although collaboration may be low, still get to know the connected link on either side of you to understand how the hand-offs can be done in a more productive way.

PARTNER: A partnership involves a low number of connections with high collaboration. Two or three people work well together to pursue an initiative or achieve a goal. There are many effective partnerships, especially in niche areas. In smaller markets or defined segments, collaboratively working with a few people can make a difference quickly and effectively. Expanding outside a defined area may challenge this model as more people will need to be involved to gain greater momentum and a broader reach.

Law firms or accounting practices are often designed and implemented this way. Two or three lawyers might partner on the same case.

Here are key questions for you and your team members:

- How can diversity of viewpoints and contributions add value to your work?

- How can diversity of viewpoints and contribution strengthen the decisions to be made?

- How would broader engagement create more momentum for your initiatives?

If your work has a strict focus or smaller target audience, then finding the right partner to do the work and have an impact may be the ideal approach. Many connections may just distract so build a tight partnership to create the right solutions and gain the right productive results.

COLLABORATIVELY ENGAGED: These are big causes and initiatives with the greatest potential for return and impact. With a high number of connections and a high level of collaboration, a lot can be accomplished, but projects at this level require leadership and coordination. To achieve big results and broad reach, more people need to work well together—collaboratively, interdependently, and fully engaged.

Here are key questions for you and your team members:

- How can you sustain your collaborative levels over time?

- What are you doing to identify the right connections to leverage at the right time?

- What can you do to retain the engagement level of as many individuals as possible while adding in more to foster greater momentum and results?

Ask, convince, and inspire as many connections as possible to move to a Level 5 Champion level and then foster effective collaboration to sustain the engagement level and gain momentum.

To achieve this, a leader clarifies purpose, mission, and responsibilities constantly. And builds trust always.

When you engage at Level 4 or Level 5, determine the engagement level required and the right collaborative approach. Getting participating individuals aligned in their engagement level will deliver a better collaborative environment.

THE BOLD NECESSITY OF TRANSPARENCY

How do you assure that everyone on a Collaboratively Engaged Project is a Champion? One word: Transparency. Put transparency at the center of the Collaborative Mix. Transparency makes work productive, seamless, and timely.

Collaboration's success depends upon how transparent we are with our team members and investors—how work is done, how and what words are spoken, and how the results are accounted for. Without transparency, collaboration falls apart quickly and, sometimes, irreparably.

THE COLLABORATIVE MIX

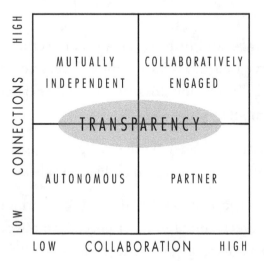

Transparency plays a key role in partnering wise patience with impassioned impatience.

- Working AUTONOMOUSLY requires high transparency with one's self.

- Working MUTUALLY INTERDEPENDENTLY requires hearty transparency between others to empower their independent work as well as to enable smooth and confident hand-offs.

- Working in a PARTNERSHIP requires transparency between you and your partner—thoroughly and completely.

- Working COLLABORATIVELY requires extraordinary transparency to keep pace in achieving milestones and realizing the ultimate mission and goals.

Transparency is a vital component for effective Millennial leadership.

Collaboratively Engaged is the new project model to achieve big things. Each quadrant may have a place from time to time, but fully engaged collaboration will have a broader and more sustainable impact. Creating strong, interdependent relationships provides a strengthened root system to engage and collaborate in more meaningful and effective ways.

THE CODE OF TRANSPARENCY

Millennial leaders who embrace **the code of transparency** to facilitate effective collaboration will build stronger teams and produce better results.

1. COLLABORATE WITH EMPATHY.

Most expressive Millennials don't want cold-hearted, emotionless peers. They expect to work with real human beings with real feelings. The tricky thing to negotiate as a Millennial leader is not to create an environment that goes to the other extreme of "cold-hearted": an emotional maelstrom free-for-all.

Empathy turns out to be a Millennial leader's powerful resource of emotional intelligence. It demands you occasionally dismantle your self-centered filters. It asks you to listen to collaborators, sense what isn't being said, and imagine how a project must look from their view point.

We've all been there: Talking with a colleague, you sense something is bothering him, but you leave it unasked. You'd rather not deal with emotions. Then, fearing his reaction, you hold back, and you don't fully share your thoughts or position. These are not transparent moments, and they are not empathetic ones either. As a result, a lot of internal "storytelling" wheels turn in a collaborator's mind that can misdirect their efforts and stall a project.

A non-Millennial entrepreneur had a software product in prototype stage. His team had reached finals in an investment contest that, if they won, could have translated to their attaining a few million dollars to develop the product. As their next deadline loomed, emotions flared. Team members started taking out their emotions with subtle personal attacks and with blaming one another for costly errors and delays. He was ill-equipped to cope with the inevitable emotional challenges that ensue in group dynamics. The Old School approach encourages people to bury emotions and move on. The New School encourages a brave emotional intelligence especially among leaders.

When you cultivate empathy as a leader, you attune to how you speak, act, and engage. Listening to understand what another person is saying is the only way to find common points to leverage your team's potential. Talking in a way to be understood and heard delivers the right tone for collaboration. Acting to ensure others are involved in meaningful ways that engage their unique talents produces real collaborative results.

Empathy is being transparent in what we convey and in what we receive. Effective collaboration requires openness; otherwise, time is wasted dancing around an issue or concern without resolving it. Leaders take the extra step and ask the questions to get to the real issues. Speak your unsaid thoughts and emotions. This is bold transparency.

Empathy activates transparency and clarifies which issues need resolution.

2. LAY OUT A TRANSPARENT MAP.

Transparency means there are no secrets. All is known about direction, pitfalls, challenges, benchmarks, performance, and more. Everything necessary to run an organization is out in the open so everyone knows where everything stands.

Do you think organizations and teams can handle radical transparency? Do you think they can be really open to the goals, objectives, challenges, mistakes, and successes? Do you think organizations and teams would operate better if this openness were present?

I know so. I've witnessed it succeed. Transparency equals clarity. Clarity equals focused actions. Transparency enables interdependent leaders and may strike fear into independent, self-centered ones.

Transparency makes sense. When secrets disappear, politics evaporate with them. Personal maneuvering and internal positioning go away since the leader shines a light on all successes, missteps, and failures. With transparency, trust happens and everyone involved beams more brightly in both attitude and participation. They become Champions—of the project, of themselves, and of one another.

Social media enables transparency. When mishaps or missteps occur, it usually shows up in someone's Facebook timeline or Twitter stream with no delay. From here, the news spreads quickly. Social media enables a certain honesty and trust in the world today. Transparency enforces accountability.

Online work stations such as centraldesktop.com and asana.com and Basecamp.com let all team members see one another's tasks and responsibilities as well as any virtual work space correspondence. In this way, no team member feels "left out" or as if other team members are conspiring against him or her.

Collaboration requires good working relationships, and transparency ensures everyone knows what each is working on as well as the status of required actions. Transparency enables collaborative partners to focus on the work to be done and eliminates much personal drama and challenges.

As a leader, adopt transparency. It will strengthen everyone's trust in your leadership abilities.

3. PROGRESS ON PURPOSE.

People give their best effort when they know their actions have a greater collective purpose. People become disengaged when leaders are self-centered. Without a focused higher purpose, people get distracted, and efforts get misdirected.

It sounds obvious to you. You're a leader. You know what the purpose is. You know what the greater vision is. Your challenge, though, is to share that purpose and vision effectively and repeatedly. With high-engagement projects, you make progress when you align progress between two points— where your team is and where you want them to be.

Transparency empowers progress. Simply put, your role as leader is periodically but not pedantically to remind your team of your collective mission and how each person's role contributes to the greater good. Once everyone champions the same purpose, each person can better filter which actions are distracting (not contributing to the purpose) and which actions are useful (contributing to the purpose).

Create effective strategic plans and run meetings in purposeful, interactive, and results-oriented ways. Create accountability by using the Code of Transparency. With empathy, foster mutual accountability wherein people accept responsibility for what goes well and not so well. Accountable moments are learning ones that produce growth in skills and capabilities.

Extreme clarity of purpose keeps everyone centered. If your team seems to run in distracted activity, check in and assure everyone remembers the purpose. If progress is thwarted or stuck, review actions, identify accountability points, and make the changes required.

Aspens embody a well-rooted story of successful collaboration. No aspen stands alone. The effectiveness of collaboration is based on sound qualities we can adopt as principles: interdependence, engagement, transparency, and purpose.

Collaboration built on these principles runs much more deeply into your group's root system so to speak than if you based your collaboration methods only on process and "how-to" methods. Get your collaborative principles right, and your approach will become inner-driven and intuitive.

ASPEN ACTIONS

In your leadership practices, engage the following Aspen Actions:

- Ensure that your Champion engagement level for specified projects and causes is aligned with your core beliefs and purpose.

- Review your connections to ensure diversity of insight and capability. Evaluate your connections to determine where the collaborative relationships can spring and be leveraged. Write down names and begin to move the connections to a collaborative, actively engaged state.

- Identify ways for your team members and colleagues to collaborate in more open and full ways. Challenge your organizational culture and determine how your actions can lead the way.

- Collaborate with transparency. Have clarity of goals, actions, and responsibilities. Hold yourself accountable along with others. Practice having real conversations with empathy and transparency.

ASPEN TRUTH 3
SPUR PURPOSE

Purpose is about positioning yourself
and others for soul sparks,
igniting aspirational leadership.

We know purpose drives Millennials. In the <u>2013 Millennial Impact Report</u>, an astonishing seventy-three percent of Millennials volunteered for a nonprofit organization.[9] They acted from passion, said seventy-nine percent, and

---

9   2013 Millennial Impact Report, Achieve and The Case Foundation.

sixty-seven percent believed they could make a difference. You are truly out to change the world.

Ryan Schoenike is no different. While watching a documentary on the national debt, he decided to give his time and resources to drive a change. Ryan co-founded <u>The Can Kicks Back</u> in order to raise awareness that the burden of the fiscal crisis falls squarely on the Millennial generation. The Can Kicks Back is engaged in efforts to get legislators to take action now to resolve our financial problems. This is the Millennial generation in action—full of purpose and out to change age-old problems with a new mindset.

WHAT'S THE CAUSE?

Millennials want to be part of big change. You don't want to wait "your turn" to make a difference, which is why many Millennials are turning away from government service jobs and turning toward nonprofits and entrepreneurship. Through nonprofits, Millennials can have a more immediate impact. In 2013 research conducted for Harvard's Institute of Politics, fifty-three percent of college students volunteered and forty-one percent served at least a few times a month.[10] In a 2011 study completed by the Affluence Collaborative, forty percent of Millennials have started, or expect to start, a business.[11] Their entrepreneurship rate is ten percent higher than the general population.

This drive for big impact also leads to newer business models that weave purpose and profit. There will likely be a growth in one-for-one business models like TOMS and Warby Parker or other conscious-oriented models. Purpose is a central motivator for Millennials, whether profit or non-profit.

Purpose and profits mix well together just as do connections and collaboration. Companies like TOMS and Warby Parker understand the power of each, which leads their community to feel more empowered by participating in the purpose. Purpose teases out of people better engagement, and effective leaders seize this opportunity.

---

10   Survey of Young Americans' Attitudes Toward Politics and Public Service: 23rd Edition, Institute of Politics, Harvard University, April 30, 2013, page 16.

11   Gary Swart, "Welcome To The New Millennial Economy: Goodbye Ownership, Hello Access, Forbes, October 11, 2012.

Without a strong sense of purpose in the work being done, individuals become stuck in routines. Work becomes mundane. Without a strong sense of purpose, teams become more politicized or self-involved. Teams become distracted. Without a strong sense of purpose, organizations lose focus and creative edge. Businesses slip market share and competitiveness.

If you want to activate your innate potential as a Millennial leader, consider how you can drive peers and teams by helping them recognize a project's or initiative's larger cause. To do so might not be as easy as it sounds. But it is possible if you tap into your potential on purpose.

- How do you know your own purpose as a leader?

- How will Millennials inspire others to join in their cause-centered initiatives?

- How will you sustain your cause-engaged leadership? How will team members and colleagues sustain their engagement?

ASPEN TRUTH #3

Aspens support their surrounding ecosystems that extend beyond the aspens themselves. Their bark contains medicinal value, an aspirin-like quality that is used by animals and humans alike. Native Americans used aspens to heal eyes and ears. The bark protects the tree from the sun and when refined can serve as a natural sun screen to human skin.

In other words, aspens benefit more than just themselves and the grove of aspens itself.

If the people you lead operate like an aspen grove, then your efforts also ultimately serve a community or cause beyond your team's or business's immediate benefit. If cause-centered, you and your collaborators nurture an ecosystem of sorts for the long-term.

As a Millennial leader, heed this ASPEN TRUTH #3: Spur Purpose. Purpose involves positioning yourself and others for soul sparks, igniting aspirational leadership. The Activate Leadership approach essentially helps you activate your innate passion for purpose in three branches.

1. LEAD FROM YOUR INTERNAL PURPOSE.

Understanding your purpose can take years of experience, yet you can accelerate refining your sense of purpose by deliberately taking advantage of appropriate opportunities and engaging your talents. Through both reflecting and acting intentionally, you discover your innate purpose. With a more clearly defined internal purpose, you can lead other Millennials with more conviction and clarity to fight, create, and make things for big impact.

2. INCLUDE THE GREATER COMMUNITY.

Think of the networks of people geographically near you and your business. Think of the networks of people related to or complementary to your business that you have forged connections with. These networks of people are your, your team's, your business's ecosystem. If you're clear not only about your personal purpose but also about the cause for which you stand, then you will be clear about how your team's efforts nurture that greater ecosystem.

A business's or venture's sustainable strength comes from a solid foundation built on community-building. From this base, you can reach beyond your immediate business borders and serve with greater ability and confidence. Include some of the people near you—in your neighborhood, office space, friend-circle. Balance the time you spend in virtual space with live time.

Connecting—a concerned look, a warm handshake, or an excited voice—fosters our human need for community and can inspire your virtual interactions in more meaningful ways. Similarly, virtual connections can encourage people to gather in a physical space, getting together to exchange words and lend a hand.

3. INSPIRE & ASPIRE: ALIGN YOUR PURPOSE WITH THE GREATER CAUSE.

Once you get clear about your current personal purpose and forge solid connections with your greater ecosystem, you as a Millennial leader can better align your purpose with your venture's greater cause. Like aspens, you and your team get strengthened by your nourishing communities beyond your business borders.

ACTIVATE LEADERSHIP

1. LEAD FROM YOUR INTERNAL PURPOSE.

When I was young, I rarely thought about time. It felt infinite, like I could do anything at any time. The reality is, life is short. If you live to be ninety-five, you have 34,675 days.

By eighteen, you've used up 6,570 of those days. None of us know exactly how many days we have in our life.

In many respects, it took me a couple of adult-working decades to get super-clear about my greater purpose and cause for leadership. You can shave some distracted years off by reflecting and acting on purpose sooner than later.

The point: Don't let your time slip away by doing wasteful things. Don't waste your time leading by pissing people off. Don't waste your time doing things that lack integrity. Leading without principles will leave you empty inside. Take your time to figure out how to make the most of it. Take your time and figure out how to make people around you better and accomplish more. Take your time, but don't invest too much in just thinking about it.

Purpose answers the question: **"Why am I doing this?"** If the answer leaves you hollow, then you haven't found the right answer yet.

These questions can help clarify your purpose:

- How do you want to be remembered?

- Within your home, and your family?

- Within your workplace?

- Within your community?

Yes, I want to be remembered as a good dad and as someone who provided a solid foundation on which my sons can live out their purpose. Added to this, I want to leave something behind that others will bring forward, think about, act upon, and make better. My written words fill a part of this purpose, but bringing them to life by what I do and how I do it matter as much, if not more. With this as my standard, I have set the bar high in what I should be doing each day and week. Within my time, momentum from each word spoken or written and action taken should lift up my purpose. This is more than about me; it is how I spark something in others.

Purpose, like an internal engine and guide, generates energy and will help you navigate challenging times with greater clarity. Get clear in your purpose and you will lead faster and more efficiently than those who flounder in a lost sense of purpose well into their forties and fifties.

Life is short. This one task—get clear on purpose—may be the biggest time-saver in your life's work. Purpose helps you weave through the barriers; it lifts you up when you are tired; and it keeps you centered when distractions and questions arise. Today and every day, live and lead the memory you want to leave behind.

This is purpose. Know yours.

2. INCLUDE THE GREATER COMMUNITY.

When we think of "community," we think neighborhoods and immediate surrounding areas. These are the places we live, eat, gather, learn, and engage. Today, community takes on a larger role as social networks expand our reach and enhance the diversity of our "neighbors."

In work, community plays a key role as well. Community at work includes our colleagues, partners, investors, customers, and competitors. Unfortunately, many times we don't think of work as a community, but a change is underway. Traditional stakeholder mindsets are being replaced with a free-flowing community view, more easily understanding the critical nature of all "citizens" and involving them in more purposeful ways.

Work spaces are being designed with community in mind. Communal areas are popular places within an office building to work and collaborate. With wireless connectivity, we can engage and work anywhere, including coffee shops, airports, cars. Community at work delivers a window to new collaborative relationships along with a greater need to understand and deliver on purpose.

More than your network, community expands what you and your team members can achieve. There are three real elements to this:

1. WHAT YOU DO OUTSIDE YOUR WORKPLACE

2. WHOM YOU SERVE IN YOUR COMMUNITY AT WORK

3. HOW YOU TREAT YOUR TEAMS AND COLLEAGUES

Encouraging people within your workplace to do something outside their daily work expands their perspective and enhances their empathy skills. Community delivers a larger context for what we do and the impact we have (or possibly can have). What you do outside your workplace will strengthen your work and perspective within your work space.

The same is true for the community within and surrounding your business and organization. I work at a healthcare software company in the marketing department. Staying within the confines of this space limits my perspective. I can develop a brand and lead generation programs to entice health IT professionals to consider our software. All good. However, how inspiring is this work?

When I expanded outside of this limited view, I began to see what patient engagement and health literacy means. A broader view creates inspiration plus more. One way I did this was by bringing a patient advocate, Regina Holliday, to our user conference. Regina lost her husband through a disease and a disconnected health care system. As Regina told her story, a silence set in, absorbing her message and knowing through our near-tears the greater purpose we try to serve each day.

Context delivers inspiration of why our work is not mundane. A larger community perspective delivers this context.

The other element of community is how you treat others. Do no harm is simply a powerful way to lead. Many forget this and focus on pettiness instead. Doing no harm, though, is a very minimal community standard. How do you leave a community or team better than it was before you arrived? Teams are just smaller communities. Organizations are a group of teams within a larger community of suppliers, partners, investors, and customers. How you treat your communities says a lot about you as a person and leader.

Your influence will grow as you trust and help others. An essential question of leadership is "How do you make others better?" When you help others become better contributors and leaders, you will become a better leader, too.

3. INSPIRE AND ASPIRE: ALIGN YOUR PURPOSE WITH THE GREATER CAUSE.

If you're grounded and rooted in your beliefs and sense of purpose, you'll be able to motivate your team with greater authenticity.

You are a motivator. You are a coach. Get equipped to stoke others when they're down. As a leader, that's part of your job description. That means you have to be other-oriented. If you're cultivating empathy as we defined with Aspen Truth #2—Connect to Expand, Collaborate to Create—then you can build on that emotional intelligence when you must motivate yourself and your team.

To do so, know the difference between inspiring yourself and others and aspiring.

TO INSPIRE is to convey a feeling of joining a higher cause, influencing soulful action.

TO ASPIRE is to rise up to a great plan, an abundant hope of fulfilling a worthwhile mission.

Know when and how to inspire and when and how to aspire. Do both wisely, and you'll spur your team to a greater cause that will mean something to them and to your business ecosystem.

POSITION FOR SOUL SPARKS

As a motivational leader, inspire others. And yourself. When collaborating on high-engagement projects, we all need a spark. Leaders are not exempt. Seek inspiration to re-orient yourself when you lose your way.

Tap into sources of inspiration. How? First, figure out where your soul sparks come from. And then determine where your team members can catch their soul sparks. A team that excels is a team that sparks together!

SOUL SPARKS are those small ignitions of inspiration that fan into big changes, new directions, or fresh works. They come from deep down inside. Make your body and mind shake with excitement. These are soul sparks.

Soul sparks guide purpose-driven leadership; they reveal what you want to Champion. Without a soul spark, you or any team member will likely never engage at a Champion level. Being an engaged, collaborative leader requires steadily firing soul sparks.

Leading with purpose requires a fire from within along with a sustaining force and reason to continue forward when all seems impossible. Soul sparks keep your leadership mindset open and strong.

A soul spark is changing the way you hold meetings because you learned the value of huddles at a conference. A soul spark is a new idea that happened during listening to a concert you may not have really wanted to take the time for. A soul spark is seeing a light return to someone's eyes because you listened well and offered words of counsel. Soul sparks can change you and others.

For me, soul sparks can come during a run in the park, listening to my thoughts and latching on to the ones that count. They come in engaging, thought-filled conversations, lingering ideas keep coming back to me. Soul sparks come at the events I attend. Afterwards, an unexpected new path appears, more convincing than the one I was on.

There are four types of soul sparks:

PERSONAL SOUL SPARKS —Personal Souls Sparks inspire initiatives in your work and outside of work. They could be charitable activities, writing projects, or other things that are, well, personal. What delivers personal satisfaction? A true sense of meaning to you? What makes you unique in what you do and say?

To make your work life sing, take time to recharge your existing soul sparks and ignite new ones. Personal soul sparks are about flow—finding those moments of joy in and out of work that make you smile and stir up your inner spirit. Personal soul sparks are as important to you as to others within your organization. Everyone needs to keep refreshed to deliver the highest impact.

For individuals in your teams and organizations, inquire about what they enjoy doing outside of work. Encourage them to discover those outside activities that put a smile on their face. By doing this, they will bring that joy inside their team work and add new creativity and collaboration to the activities ahead.

If out of rhythm, then try the following:

- Find the time to explore new interests outside of work.

- Encourage others to get involved in community work or pursue a creative talent.

- Live the example of a complete life—inside and outside of work.

RELATIONSHIP SOUL SPARKS —Relationships include your friends, boyfriend, girlfriend, partner, spouse, parents, co-workers, kids, and others. These are the people who spark a fire in you, now and again, make you better, and you, them. The people who hold you up when you need support; love you when you are down; challenge you when you are sliding by; and hold you accountable when you slip off track.

Relationship soul sparks inspire core friendships and spirited conversations. Engaging conversations matter. They make you think and engage your soul. Really good conversations will refresh you. Relationship soul sparks connect your words to actions and actions to accountability.

Finding a group of people outside of work may deliver this spark. I started a monthly Meetup group in which leaders at all levels from different industries gather to share experiences, lifting us all up in how we solve problems and keep our teams engaged. But don't just focus on the outside. Develop the relationships within your business that can serve as a source of learning and inspiration.

If you're not developing new connections and relationships, then try the following:

- Start a group of leaders to meet monthly and discuss topics of interest.

- Volunteer to help out regularly at a local school, charity, or other community initiative.

- Suggest ways for others to get involved in local trade groups like American Marketing Association, Social Venture Partners, and alumni organizations.

- Have lunch each week with someone from a different department or team.

LEADERSHIP SOUL SPARKS—These sparks are the ones that give you a sense of direction in how to lead an organization, initiative, or team. Leadership soul sparks enliven your passion to move things forward, upward, over the humps, and across the distances. They deliver more than enlightened leadership; they also define your determination while spurring your abilities to work with people.

Leadership soul sparks lift all up to achieve new things. They activate aspirations and enhance clarity of what needs to get done. They improve or revamp your leadership capabilities.

A recent soul spark for me came while reading a book by Dr. Henry Cloud entitled *Integrity: The Courage to Meet the Demands of Reality* and taking an online course from the Willow Creek Association. The question raised that reverberated through me was, "What wake are you leaving in your path?" This spark stung.

Workplace politics arise anywhere so I am not exempt. A few years ago, we were making some changes to an online customer community and needed the support and insights from key groups. However, for whatever reasons, certain groups were sitting on the sidelines but with implicit disgruntlement. At first, I ignored their implicit criticism. After all, at times, it seems more stress-free to just complete the work and roll past certain people.

Leaving issues unaddressed is easy but leaves a messy wake. I was guilty. I needed to change. I took Dr. Cloud's advice and went, "soft on the person but hard on the issue." As a leader, I realized I could not afford to leave issues for someone else to deal with. I needed to be a better leader. By addressing the issue head on, I didn't leave a disgruntled person behind. Instead, I solved a problem and gained deeper support on an essential initiative. This is the power of leadership soul sparks—guiding us to be better leaders.

Leadership skills and abilities get stale if left alone. That's dangerous. Learning invigorates. New experiences energize. New connections expand empathy. Each refreshes your leadership capabilities. Seek leadership sparks.

If you're developing a fixed leadership mindset, then try the following:

- Identify new books to read or start a book club within your organization.

- Encourage your team members to attend trade conventions or other conferences to expand views and learn new things.

- Implement new practices with your team, whether it is how you facilitate meetings or conduct performance appraisals—change your leadership practices in positive ways.

CAREER SOUL SPARKS —Work is part of living. Finding work that thrills us is often a challenge. Career soul sparks is that feeling or voice or jolt inside that, when listened to, sounds like what we want to spend our working hours doing fully and passionately.

Career soul sparks happen when we are teens, setting a direction for college. They happen during our professional life and can set a new direction at times. They are the sources that keep our work on a purposeful track rather than looping in lifeless circles.

My first career spark was attending Boys State, an American Legion program for select high school students to learn about citizenship and government. This experience sparked a major in political science and over seven years working in Washington, DC, starting as a legislative assistant for a U.S.

Senator, and finally working in Eisenhower Old Executive Office Building for a deputy assistant to the president in The White House.

My second spark came through getting my MBA and inspired a fifteen-plus-year career in marketing and technology. I didn't know where my career sparks would come from, and you may not either. Keeping your career sparks going is challenging as you age. Our careers get surrounded by family responsibilities, home ownership, and other boundaries that pop up. Too often, everyone gets buried in in what we need to do instead of what we could do.

As a leader, part of your role is to position yourself in different opportunities. To gain career growth, learn, take on new projects, resolve tough problems, and untangle difficult working relationships. No matter the challenge, listen to the spark. It will enhance your career path.

Do the same for your team members. Provide new projects and initiatives for them to take the lead on. Break them free from their normal daily activities and see what you can unleash by giving them a bigger project to undertake or tougher problem to solve. This isn't about working them harder; this is about giving them the opportunity to catch a career spark through gaining greater autonomy, delivering bigger impacts, collaborating with new teams, and building constructive relationships.

If you're becoming stale in a career, then try the following:

- Volunteer for new assignments or challenging projects.

- Tap team members to solve a new problem or be a team lead on a new initiative.

- Break out of normal routines and catch a new stride.

Soul sparks. You cannot lead or live well without them. Your team needs them.

Just as aspens reach out, so must you. There is no greater gift you can give someone else within your organization, team, or community than an opportunity to experience a spark. This may sound simplistic, but can you imagine an organization leading fully in purpose? Talk about Level 5 engagement! The result will be an inspired group of people changing things to help achieve results for your organization and the surrounding community. The two are not mutually exclusive. Like the aspens—lead with purpose where you stand and then beyond your reach.

Soul sparks alone are not enough, however. We cannot lead and live on inspiration alone. More is needed to sustain us on our purpose-driven path.

LEADERS SPUR PURPOSE AND CAUSE.

Have you ever looked around a room or community and seen one person more alive with what he or she is doing? Others seem drawn to him or her because the person savors value-rich conversation and to help out in whatever way possible. These people are leaders who exude purpose. They provide an extra oomph to the team who comes in range of their passion. More, they can see the big picture. They can tell you how selling cars is tied with a bigger cause of building human relationships. They can show you how designing websites is furthering good missions across the globe. This person is you.

With Aspen Truth #1—Patience Cultivates Growth—you defined and claimed your core beliefs. Let those core beliefs be the nutrient-rich root system from which your team purpose and cause extend.

When our beliefs align with our purpose, we have staying power in what we are doing and how we are leading. Most importantly, purpose and cause engage actions in a space greater than our own survival needs.

Purpose is not a private solo venture. It blooms from a solid foundation of core beliefs, an open soul, and an out-reaching mindset.

In this noisy world, let the call to serve and lead with purpose be an essential part of your work and actions. From here, greater impact unfolds.

Activate your innate leadership potential by combining inspirational soul sparks with aspirational big picture mapping.

INSPIRE AND ASPIRE: DIGGING DEEPER

A disconnect happens when inspire and aspire stand alone. By itself, to inspire a team can be inert. It's like a motivational speech with no plan. A stirring inside to lead or participate, stirred-up and not acted on, leads nowhere.

A team that aspires alone also can be limiting. Inside, we feel good about what we are thinking and moving forward with, but, without inspiration from others, the actions lose luster. Aspiration isn't about always needing an audience for what we desire to do; it is about how organizations and communities are needed to make things happen in real, meaningful ways.

Joining aspire and inspire create vitality of purpose.

THE VITALITY OF PURPOSE

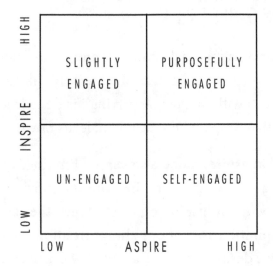

UN-ENGAGED. If both inspiration and aspiration are missing in your leadership, you lose soul. You become un-engaged and, worse, disengaged. Being un-engaged in a leadership position will weigh on everyone; they will dread work and culture.

SELF-ENGAGED. Those leaders highly aspired but with little inspiration are self-engaged. Some people have an inner drive and are comfortable pursuing large goals without much inspiration coming in or flowing out. Yet if as leader you only drive yourself and do not inspire others, you become a figurine: you stand for many to see but no one to hear.

Being self-engaged can lead to frustration, dashed hopes, delayed dreams. Ron Johnson, the former CEO of JCPenney, may fit in this quadrant. He aspired to instigate big changes in the way the stores looked, flowed, and were merchandized. While he had big dreams of possibility, others weren't necessarily inspired. As time wore on, people became worn out, and Ron Johnson was fired.

SLIGHTLY ENGAGED. Only being inspired with little sense of aspiration means you feel the passion, yet you wallow in emotion. There is no action to bring your unique talents and big ideas or thoughts to life. You sit on the sidelines, soaking it all in, and avoid getting fully into the arena of meaningful activity. Slightly engaged leadership is a waste.

Carly Fiorina, former CEO of HP, is an interesting example here. Her action at HP could be classified as inspiring. She made bold moves to acquire and consolidate Compaq into their product offerings. However, without greater clarity of the larger purpose, team members became less committed, and analysts less enthused. There was an established "HP Way"—as defined by the early co-founders, Bill Hewlett and David Packard—and Carly's inspired actions weren't enough to usher in a new way. A new, aspiring way wasn't defined. Full engagement, a more compelling vision, and refreshed principles were needed.

PURPOSEFULLY ENGAGED. When we add in the right mix of inspiration and aspiration, something magical happens. Purpose ensues! We have lofty goals and a meaningful mission. What we aspire to do stirs inspiration in others to join in. Being open to be inspired is fuel for your aspirations.

Howard Schultz, CEO of Starbucks, may fit into the Purposefully Engaged quadrant. He goes out of his way to ensure the customer experience is exceptional. This mission shows up in employee training and in their designs. Beyond the storefront, Howard Schultz instigates campaigns like "Come Together" to encourage legislators to find common ground and solve important national issues, or "Pay It Forward" encourages customers in small acts of kindness—buying a cup of coffee for a stranger. He mixes inspiration and aspiration to lead well within his organization and within a larger community.

Jason Fried, CEO of Basecamp (formerly 37Signals), may fit here, too. Basecamp creates software to help other companies manage their projects. Basecamp is one of their popular solutions. What Jason does is more than create software, though. He also shares experiences with the desire to help other leaders and entrepreneurs. Many believe bigger to be better, but Jason thinks it's okay for companies to be smaller, built for the long term; he inspires a different approach.

Jason is Purposefully Engaged. He works to share his thoughts and experiences and encourages others to think again about what is important in building a business. He said recently, "I'd like to give back as much as I can, but I don't just want to give something to say I'm giving back. I really want to figure out what it is that I can help with in a much bigger way. I don't know if I've really hit that yet."[12] Leading by showing how culture can trump big growth and how building a business can be done in an out-of-ordinary formula is Jason at his best.

Another example is Tony Hsieh, chief executive officer at Zappos.com. Tony has been at the forefront of what culture means for an organization. In his book, *Delivering Happiness: A Path to Passion, Profits, and Purpose*, he awakened leaders to a new way to think about their organizational culture. Tony and the great people at Zappos.com have delivered more than happiness; they have been delivering high-performing, customer-centered results. Together,

---

12   Jason Fried, The Great Discontent, Interview by Tina Essmaker, May 1, 2013.

they are inspiring other leaders and organizations to build companies in better ways.

Tony is not resting here. He recently announced a move to a new organizational structure called <u>Holocracy</u>, which eliminates traditional hierarchical structures and distributes power to the many and to a constitution. This approach is transformational, and Tony is continuing to lead in a way that encourages other leaders to engage new models to empower people.

In tandem, aspiration and inspiration work amazingly well together. When one is weak, the stronger one pulls the other up. When both are robust, anything can be accomplished.

This is leadership afire with purpose, and this is your call. Leading with purpose is the call of the aspens to embrace your embedded purpose so you spur others to a larger, meaningful cause.

Aspens nourish their greater ecosystem. Tapping into your purposeful flow may take more effort, but your impact will be greater than if you act without core purpose.

ASPEN ACTIONS

In your leadership practices, engage the following Aspen Actions to activate Aspen Truth #3—Spur Purpose:

- Take the time to understand your purpose. Write it down. Don't wait. Time is limited, life finite. Don't rush understanding your purpose, but carve out the time to explore and be present in what your talents are. After you write your purpose down, put it into action each week. Lead from that core purpose.

- Determine ways to position yourself for soul sparks—personal, relationship, leadership, and career. The practices do not need to be complex. They can be as simple as a weekly walk in the park with a close friend, spouse, or partner, or reading a weekly article on leadership. Carve out the time. Be open.

- Determine ways to position others on your team for soul sparks. Encourage them to attend lunch events with a guest speaker or offer opportunities for them to attend virtual or local training. Find ways to create a reason for others to be inspired.

- Combine leading to inspire and to aspire. Ensure your purpose-driven leadership has a vitality behind it, bringing others along and empowering others to help out. Connect the dots for your team between their daily actions and the greater cause you collectively are reaching for.

ASPEN TRUTH 4
CONVERT TO THRIVE

EFFECTIVELY CONVERTING INFORMATION
AND DIVERSE VIEWPOINTS INTO ACTION
WILL DISTINGUISH YOU AS A LEADER.

When <u>Emily Rolla</u>[13] entered college, she thought she was headed for a sure job in public relations or social media management. But she graduated into the United States's most prolonged period of economic agony since the Great Depression. After trying about eight months to get a job in her field of study, Emily finally accepted a retail job at Target.

---

13   Lynn LeCluyse, "Millennials, young minority adults suffer high rates of unemployment," *Catholic News Service*, August 12, 2013.

Thirty-seven percent of eighteen-to-twenty-nine year-olds are unemployed or out of the workforce, the highest in more than thirty years. Being unemployed for more than twenty-six weeks can have devastating effects on earnings and careers for nearly twenty years afterwards (*Federal Reserve Bank of Boston study*, January 2014).[14] This economic impact translates to Millennials having to do more than survive. They have to find wise strategies to thrive.

It turns out that your capacity to thrive in this climate depends in part on your ability to convert. Quickly and on purpose.

ADAPTABLE, CONFIDENT MILLENNIALS

The blow of these economic conditions is as large as your generation. According to NPR's *Educated And Jobless: What's Next For Millennials?*, in 2011[15]

---

14   Daniel Cooper, "The Effect of Unemployment Duration on Future Earnings and Other Outcomes," **Federal Reserve Bank of Boston**, January 13, 2014.

15   "Educated And Jobless: What's Next For Millennials?" NPR, November 12, 2011.

- Only fifty-five percent of Millennials had a job.

- A quarter of people between ages twenty-five and thirty-four were living with their parents.

- Individuals under thirty-five are worth 68% less than people of the same age twenty-five years ago.

The situation was bleak. However, in a study two years later by Fidelity Investments, fifty-two percent of Millennials described themselves as generally "confident" in their financial condition, more so than other generations.[16] Why? The answer lies in the fact that Millennials adapted. According to the study, you

16   "Fidelity Research Finds Gen Y Financial Perspective the 'Most Changed' Following the 2008 Financial Crisis," Fidelity, September 4, 2013.

111

- Turned to family and friends for financial advice

- Started an emergency fund to better prepare for future downturns

- Focused on saving

You learned from the situation and adapted by becoming more knowledgeable about your finances and saving more systematically.

Survival is important, but is adapting to survive enough? Millennial leaders who take it a step further—from adapting to converting—will advance in your purpose with greater results and better timing.

- With so much information available at any moment, what will prevent you from stalling in overload and over-analysis?

- What strategy will enable you to thrive and stand out in this uncertain climate?

- How will you strengthen your leadership with diversity and tangible results?

- How can you Millennials thrive by design?

The answers might have to do with flutter and bark.

ASPEN TRUTH #4

Aspen leaves quiver at the lightest puff of air because of their flatness, shape, and perpendicular connection to the leaf stem. The flutter is a secret weapon. Because aspens thrive in mountainous climates with short growing seasons, they have less time to perform photosynthesis. The flutter allows each leaf to capture more sun in a shorter period of time.

That's efficient conversion.

Aspen bark also helps the photosynthesis process. Their grayish-to-greenish hues, unlike the crusty bark of other trees, absorb the sun's rays. The aspen bark continues the photosynthesis process into the fall.

The teamwork between the leaves and the bark nourishes and enables aspens to exist in a more expansive geographic range than other North American trees. It is a well-designed partnership that does more than foster survival; it also furthers growth and expansion.

That process translates to collaborative, productive results.

In short, aspens convert to thrive. That's ASPEN TRUTH #4: Convert to Thrive.

You have a dormant capacity to adapt and survive. Now it's time to activate that capacity into a leadership talent. The Activate Leadership approach invites you to lead with a different storyline: Efficiently convert data and differing points of view into action to catalyze momentum.

To **convert** is to change something for the better. It often involves taking data in one form and using it toward a greater end.

There are three essential branches of Aspen Truth #4 to consider and test out:

1. DIVERSE RELATIONSHIPS CREATE VALUE.

The parts of an aspen tree work together for success. The leaves and bark pull in the sun light, the roots deliver the water, and the surrounding environment gives and receives in turn. More than survival is achieved; aspens thrive. In your team, let each person play their key role. Value increases with collaboration. As an individual, discover more about yourself from listening to your heart and soul and interacting with other leaders.

By exposing yourself to different sources of "light," you have the opportunity to learn more quickly and sustain your growth. Leadership by absorbing many angles of information and inspiration builds a strengthened core capability to navigate and weather changes.

2. ACT WITH EMPATHY.

Understanding without action is waste. How you move from understanding into action sets real leaders apart. Empathetic leadership means connecting from the heart with another person. Empathetic leadership means being attentive to different perspectives and knowing oneself well.

- Understand different perspectives, accept what they have to offer, and then work together to produce a better result.

- Know yourself along with where you need to advance your capabilities and change to achieve better outcomes.

3. CONVERT TO ACHIEVE.

Aspens convert sunlight, water, and carbon dioxide into food and energy. They convert resources into tangible results. Focus on converting ideas into outcomes, words into actions. How can you convert your team's actions into tangible results? Each turn facilitates greater momentum, greater results.

ACTIVATE LEADERSHIP

1. STRENGTHEN YOUR LEADERSHIP CORE THROUGH DIVERSE POVS.

You can learn a lot about a tree's age and experience by observing the inside of a cut trunk's rings. The innermost ring shows a tree's first year of growth. Each concentric ring typically shows a tree's year of growth. Aspen rings are fainter than other trees. With the light-colored wood, the rings blend together, making it more challenging to define an aspen's age. The rings are present, just less defined. And, remember, the bark doesn't create a tough barrier to penetrate; it works to absorb light and convert light into energy.

What's remarkable about aspens is that when you activate your leadership potential, your rings of growth are present but not defined by clearly marked years. You can accelerate your own inner rings of growth by taking in more information and shining through in what you produce. Most importantly, you can blur your lines of age, similar to aspens, by lowering your barriers to learn from new sources and change as required to meet new demands.

Expand your point of view on a subject or problem. Absorb differing points of view, and convert the insights you develop into meaningful actions.

Let me explain.

YOUR POV MATTERS. Whether or not you take the time to define and be aware of your Point of View (POV), you have one. Your POV includes

- Leadership – Learned or Inherent?

- People – Motivated by Good or Self-interest?

- Political Leanings – Liberal, Conservative, or Moderate?

- Charity — Involved, Just Money, Both, or Neither?

- Health — Exercise or Not? Vegetarian, Paleo, Flexitarian, Uncertain?

You get the idea, but have you stopped for a few moments and really thought through how you view things? If not, now may be a good time to do this.

Your POV is how you view, engage, and undertake certain activities. POV is what you may naturally do, say, or think, given certain situations and encounters.

Your core beliefs support your POV, just as your purpose does. Being attentive to your POV is vital, as it serves as your core place of strength. More than this, your POV needs to be attended to so it grows in perspective, approach, and skill.

Why is being attentive to your POV essential? For several reasons. First, the environment around you will inevitably change. Deciding what to change and when to remain steadfast will be a key skill set to develop. Having a solid starting point in your POV delivers a foundation to build upon. Second, you will—*and always will need to*—grow. Every good leader does, no matter our age. Knowing your POV and challenging yourself on adding, expanding, or shifting your POV means you know where you are today and what you need to strengthen leading forward. Third, without a POV, you simply lack a position and will just blow in the wind or chase gusts like they were the next best direction. A POV sets your direction and then requires an attentive mind to discern when to change it.

Knowing your POV takes ongoing care. Growth is the goal; so, taking care by tapping new sources for learning and perspective is a necessity. Similarly, taking a break to re-gain footing and refresh your energy is needed self-care, especially in a world cluttered with a glut of information. Breaking away from it all delivers a renewed view.

All of this is about being attentive to your POV. Being at-tentive also creates a sense of self-accountability instead of looking to others for approval or validation. You know what lines you might cross, and you build in ways to prevent it. You know where you need help, and you ask for it. This is an attentive, accountable leader.

Knowing who you are and what your opportunities for growth are open you up to accepting greater diversity of interactions and insights to strengthen your core areas and uncover your blind spots. Likewise, knowing what success in your team and business looks like will let you know whether you are meeting your mission or if you need to update your operational, leadership, and business models.

What emerges are your rings of leadership growth and ability.

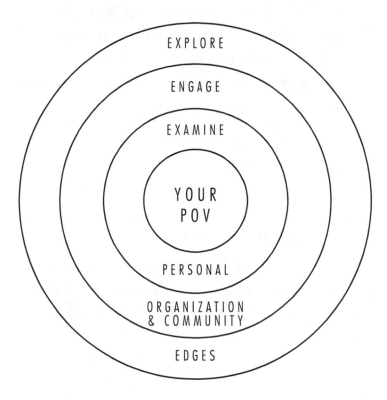

Your current leadership POV is your starting point. From here, your rings begin to expand in three primary areas.

- EXAMINE. This leadership ring keeps you attentive to your leadership abilities and assists you in the outer rings in two ways: Identifying places to engage and explore and honing your skills through personal time and reflection.

- ENGAGE. How do you challenge your current perspectives and gain new ones? The answer appears by engaging individuals with diverse views and penetrating questions. Your organization and community serve as key sources of growth.

- EXPLORE. How do you discover new thoughts or spark your creativity? The answer lies in exploration and involves getting out of your usual thought processes and takes you to the edges of new thinking or new venues for discovery.

Using your rings of leadership will expand your capabilities and keep you renewed in your views. Let's explore ways to EXAMINE, ENGAGE, and EXPLORE your rings of development.

EXAMINE

READ BIOGRAPHIES OF DIFFERENT LEADERS. If someone's life and achievements or failures resonate with you, dig deeper. Develop your library. When you feel complete studying one person, select another. Good biographies bring leadership, lessons, failures, and successes to life. They enlighten. They instruct. They engage us to select new principles and mindsets. For me, Theodore Roosevelt played this role, as did LBJ. You might select Steve Jobs while others are drawn to Andrew Carnegie or Georgia O'Keeffe. Pick someone who fascinates you to do more, learn more.

DEVELOP KEEN OBSERVER TRAITS. Watch how others address opportunities, handle big challenges, and work through problems. Observing others is as much about learning what to do as what not to do. We have the luxury of understanding others' successes and mistakes at little cost. Go to a mall and observe people. See what they notice and what their facial expressions say. Go to a hospital waiting room and witness joy and pain in others' eyes. Train yourself to observe more, learn more. The more you observe about the diversity of human beings, the better equipped you will be to empathize not only with your co-workers and teammates but also ultimately your customers and clients.

BE A GOOD CONVERSATIONALIST. People like to talk about themselves. This fact makes asking questions about others' experiences and insights a wise strategy. Being a conversationalist is not forcing questions upon people or prying into their life. Engage conversation by discussing how they got to where they are and what challenges they worked through to get there. Ask other leaders, for example, *How did you handle your various successes? How did you work through your mistakes?* Being a good conversationalist is a mix of asking good questions and listening well. Go to online forums and see what questions are being asked. Reddit or Quora are good sources.

ENGAGE

SEEK A MENTOR. Mentors open us up. Most mentors are more experienced. You hope to get perspective from someone who has industry knowledge and who's willing to advise you, look out for you, and even see the best in you and how to help move you forward.

Leverage mentorship potential when a mentor is available.

In many cases, however, you will not have a mentor. It's just a cold hard fact. Although about seventy percent of Fortune 500 companies have a mentoring program, entrepreneurial organizations will not likely have one. If there is one, the reality is it may not add a lot of value for you. However, this fact should not be a stopping point.

Finding a good mentor may take some time, but your time is well-spent here. Here are ways to find a solid mentor:

- Look outside your immediate team and identify an individual you respect because of what they have done and how they do things. This individual doesn't have to be a vice-president or a director. The person can be anyone with a strong, positive leadership POV.

- Look outside of your organization and business. Local business, industry, or community groups can be a great place to see people in action outside of their normal business hours. Getting a mentor outside of your immediate organization gives you a fresh vantage point.

- Use LinkedIn. Go through your own network and think through the relationships you have connected with. Which ones stand out? Why do they stand out? Pick someone from your network who has demonstrated the leadership capabilities you would like to strengthen yourself.

Once you have a mentor, ask a lot of questions. Explore what decisions they made in their past and the lessons learned from them. Know what their principles are and how they have served in good and bad times. Be curious about what mistakes they made and what they did to prevent them from happening again. Ask about their successes and turning points. What choices did they make to gain positive traction forward? In other words, don't be reactive in the present moment with a mentor; be proactive. Don't wait for them to always guide the conversation or deliver tidbits of wisdom. A mentor can expand your point of view, if leveraged properly and fully.

REARVIEW – OLDER GENERATIONS. Just like a root system, flow of information needs to travel in all directions in order to maintain a healthy leadership ecosystem. If the older generation doesn't want to share their insights, or accept your advice and perspective, meet the challenge: Apply subtle, excellent listening skills, and seek the right opening to engage. Empathy will help you here.

In conversations with older generations, be aware of the other person: What are they saying and how? What do they need, and how can your insight meet that need? Here are some tips:

- BE QUIET AND REFLECT BACK. Listen closely to words spoken. Notice tone. Listen for emotion. Let them finish their sentences and complete their thoughts. Listen fully. When they finish, start with,

"What I hear from you is... Is this correct?" Once clarified or confirmed, then offer your insight, question, or experience.

- WATCH FOR BODY CLUES. Are their arms open or folded? Are they comfortable or uptight? If arms are folded and the body signs are closed, then you may wish to wait for a different time, a different opportunity to offer your thoughts. Know the right timing to engage in an open and mutually beneficial way.

- INTERACT WITH UNDERSTANDING. In conveying your thoughts and perspective, don't force it. Be thoughtful in your approach. Ask questions along the way. Ask for reactions to what you offer. Hear their insights to your insights. It is in a true give-and-take interaction that your insights can be delivered and accepted.

FORWARD VIEW — ENTERING GENERATIONS. There will always be someone younger than you. Whether it is someone from Generation Z or just the younger end of your generation, someone will be starting out just like you did. Pay it forward: Give to others as you have been given. By interacting with and mentoring someone younger, your leadership insights and skills will be refreshed and honed, too. Often it is in teaching something that we understand it more fully. Listen to the younger person and let him or her serve as a reverse mentor to you.

Thriving leaders are the ones surrounded by diverse people from different generations.

EXPLORE

ATTEND A CONFERENCE. You never know what you might learn and discover. You may begin thinking about new things in new ways or old things in new ways. Put things that don't resonate aside for now; either you're not ready or they just don't fit into who you are or what you want to become. Wisdom 2.0 and Storyline are conferences that explore new ways to develop personally. Or, check out Conscious Capitalism to better understand changing business models. Be unafraid to explore creativity at the Story Chicago or BIF – Business Innovation Factory.

ATTEND PUBLIC LECTURES AT COLLEGES. There is likely a college or university within reach that has speakers and events open to the public. Go. Listen. Learn. Engage. No local university? There are many sessions online. Check out the open online courses at Yale, Harvard, and MIT, to name only a few. Coursera is another option gaining a lot of attention because it offers thousands of top-notch university courses for low tuition, and you can learn from your own computer. Just remember, you are positioning yourself to learn, grow, and improve the ways you lead, think, interact, and learn.

Being attentive to your POV and embracing diverse insights enhances your understanding and prompts you to adapt when new information or perspectives are grasped. This is empathy in action.

What begins to happen is powerful. Your leadership POV adjusts and strengthens as you tap into what each ring has to offer. As this occurs, your influence advances and widens. This is the beauty of tapping into diverse sources and using them to expand your leadership presence. This is the beauty of your natural digital photosynthesis capabilities to grow.

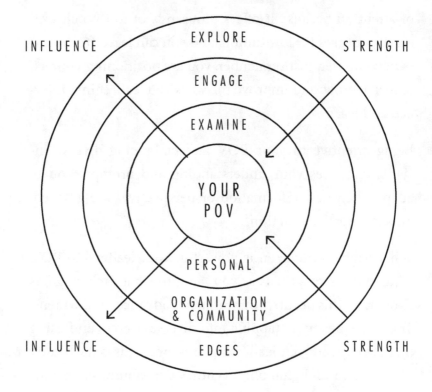

With your leadership presence more evident, now is the time to demonstrate results and, taking another aspen trait, converting is the way to achieve, make an impact, and increase your influence.

2. CONVERT TO ACHIEVE RESULTS

Now the true challenge has arrived! With a strong, pliable POV and diverse information and relationships supporting your leadership capabilities, you need to do something with your new sources of input and challenge. Having a network of information is good, but it only delivers value if you use the ABSORB-CONVERT-ACT MODEL to achieve real results, empowering you to thrive in the changing environment ahead.

The ABSORB-CONVERT-ACT MODEL helps leaders train themselves to move themselves and others from idea to action.

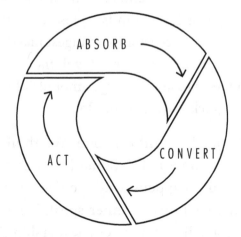

Converting well is a real difference-maker in what type of leader you will be. Change happens in a snap. One day you are on solid footing and the next day your footing disappeared because of a layoff, buy-out, or market shift in a completely different direction. Our environment is intense and complex so we must stay attuned and advance in purposeful, growth-oriented ways.

Photosynthesis means "putting together with light." Leaders of your generation don't absorb nutrients to photosynthesize. You absorb and convert. With your adaptive tendency, you will make formidable leaders, especially with an enduring focus on converting.

Let's tap into this important model.

ABSORB. We are, essentially, information sponges. Millennials' quicksilver minds, plus our Wiki-digital technology afford you the ability to ingest massive amounts of information at unprecedented volumes. An essential ability of leaders is to absorb large amounts of information in a relatively quick way, and you do.

Notice how you take in information. You think. You evaluate. You think some more. Some information lands as soul sparks. A turn happens inside you, moving from your mind toward your heart or inner spirit. When this happens, there is a call to grow your leadership POV along with how to potentially change your approach to solving a problem or adopting a different business model to address shifts in the market.

Highlighted below is a way to discern what you absorb.

1. From the information you took in, identify the big ideas, trends, or thoughts from it.

2. From the big ideas, trends, and thoughts, what filters through as the salient points to consider? Write them down.

3. From the points to consider, pinpoint the key action to move forward. Not everything will be actionable. At times, the filtered points may just remain as watch points. More information may be required to support an action so just set it as a point to watch. The Action Point may simply be to watch this big idea, trend, or thought.

ABSORB

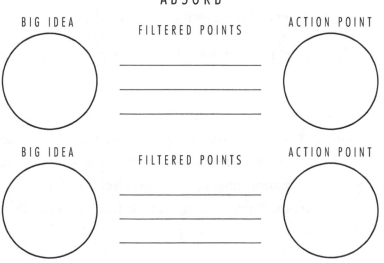

BIG IDEA   FILTERED POINTS   ACTION POINT

BIG IDEA   FILTERED POINTS   ACTION POINT

MEET THE CHALLENGES:

- BALANCE DIVERSE SOURCES OF INFORMATION: Know when enough information is enough. *Checkpoint:* When articles from different sources begin to sound the same, you may have reached a saturation point. Don't get stuck in over-absorption.

- CREATE TIME TO READ AND THINK. *Checkpoint:* Do you have a blocked, protected time to read and think? If not, carve out at least one hour per day and safeguard that time.

- IDENTIFY WHAT "STUCK" WITH YOU. The salient points remain in your thoughts for several hours or days after being read or engaged in a conversation. *Checkpoint:* Write down these filtered points.

Now let's move forward with the key step of converting what we have absorbed.

CONVERT. Absorbing information without taking action is storing it. Unless you are saving the stored data for some future reason, do something with everything you absorb. Convert information and insights into action. Take your identified Action Point and convert it into a productive, meaningful pursuit or change. Doing this will move you and your team forward.

Information converted into actionable steps can include the following:

- WRITTEN ANALYSIS

- METRICS TO TRACK

- NEW HABITS ADOPTED

- PLANS AND ACTIVITIES TO WORK AND IMPLEMENT

Think of it this way. Aspens take in sunlight and convert it into growth. As a leader, your challenge and opportunity are the same. Converting absorbed information into ways to grow, change, and thrive is what will empower you to be a stronger leader and develop better solutions.

Take what you pinpointed as the key action points and then do the following:

1. Identify key steps to take. Answer: What select actions will address the change? Define them.

2. Given the specified actions, if achieved, describe what the outcome will likely be. Create the picture of what the new result will be so others will visualize

why the change is necessary or recognize how you have changed in a positive way over time. Creating the resulting visual will incite others to become Champions in their engagement.

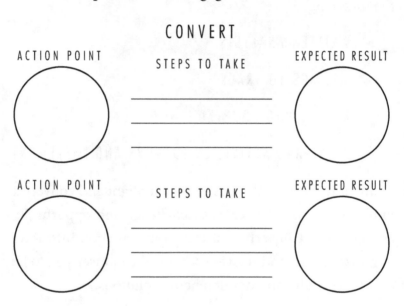

CONVERT

ACTION POINT   STEPS TO TAKE   EXPECTED RESULT

ACTION POINT   STEPS TO TAKE   EXPECTED RESULT

MEET THE CHALLENGES:

- GETTING STUCK IN OVER-ANALYSIS OR OVER PLANNING? *Checkpoint:* What have you learned by doing something with the information converted? If the answer is "nothing yet," then it is time to act— get out of your head and into your hands.

- DON'T SKIP ABSORPTION BEFORE TAKING ACTION. This could be described as "half-cocked," meaning the next steps are random and scattered. Don't let confusion be the result of your leadership. *Checkpoint:* Have you clearly identified the lessons learned or actions to take from the information absorbed? Have you documented the trends and do you understand their potential impact? If you cannot point to them in writing, stop and get clear of your next step or plan.

- ACTING FOR JUST THE SAKE OF ACTING (when work is not based on a meaningful plan): *Checkpoint:* Given your expected result, what actions will move you and others closer to it? Understand the requirements for completing the next step. If the picture of what achievement looks like is murky, stop and gain clarity.

From here, pursue what you identified as a new, better result.

ACT. After you convert information into expected results, act! Action is the movement of ideas into the world: changing, solving, doing.

Action is a requirement for being an effective leader. You influence others to do their part (and more). Taking action is about coherent and transparent pace, engagement, collaboration, and leadership.

Taking the model to the third step, define the players and time lines—who needs to collaborate and when work needs to completed. Doing this will catalyze your steps into forward motion.

ACT

EXPECTED RESULT	COLLABORATORS	TIMING

EXPECTED RESULT	COLLABORATORS	TIMING

MEET THE CHALLENGES:

- GETTING UNENGAGED OR INEFFECTIVE PEOPLE AS COLLABORATORS. *Checkpoint:* Do you have the right people engaged? Do the collaborators have the right skill sets, or do they require added training? Are they engaged at the Champion level? If not, what changes can you make to raise their engagement levels?

- ACTING TO LOOK OR FEEL BUSY. *Checkpoint:* Busyness should never be a leadership or team metric. At the end of each day, write down the three relevant and significant items you and your collaborators accomplished. If fewer than two or three, write down what you should do differently the next day and repeat.

Now it is time to put it all together. For the model to be effective, it needs to be a closed loop, meaning all three steps — ABSORB, CONVERT, ACT — are completed.

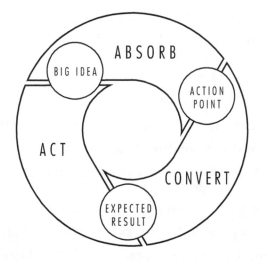

A quick example: Several years ago, in the information systems management market, our company wasn't relevant. We did not have a cohesive, meaningful story for CIOs to get excited about. The company adjusted and developed a substantial strategy, but it was difficult for our resellers to sell an enterprise solution when their customers just needed a subset of it.

Being a part of the reseller marketing team, I absorbed the new strategy along with what our resellers needed to operate effectively within their customer base. I also reviewed articles on the information systems management market from a reseller perspective. From here, the key Action Points were to make our larger strategy digestible while providing a path to expand the solution when the resellers' customers were ready. The result was a reseller strategy called "Solution Ladders."

This strategy was my converting move. This strategy not only put in place an action plan to embrace our company strategy but also made it work for our reseller partners. Our resellers loved the Solution Ladders, and they were highlighted as a sound approach in various industry articles.

Converting is a leadership skill and a leader's advantage. Converting separates the talkers from the doers and the tinkerers from the achievers. Leaders facilitate the movement of ideas, plans, and people to a motivated result. Acting in partnership with others is essential to make the magic of converting work.

Everyone is unique in their gifts and capabilities. What each of us can convert is as different as who we are. Identify what you need to move forward and then practice the act of converting.

Aspens stand out from other trees by how they absorb light in complete, productive ways and then convert it in order to grow and flourish.

Millennials have the same opportunity, as you are equipped to take in so much more than previous generations. Now the challenge is to use your collaborative nature to produce real results, real change, and real impact. I am glad to stand among your generation.

ASPEN ACTIONS

In your leadership practices, engage the following Aspen Actions:

- Identify your POV on leadership, life, business, charity, and more. Take the time to write down your POV and understand it.

- Expand your rings of growth. Be an active learner. Seek mentorship. Find people and sources to engage with. Ensure the mix is diverse — across the generations and from different points of view. Position yourself to Examine and Engage on a monthly basis.

- Identify a seminar, speaker, or conference each year that is out-of-the-ordinary for you. Leverage virtual offerings, especially if costs are a challenge. Situate yourself to gain a fresh perspective and be open to new ideas. After attending, consider what you learned and what you can apply to the work you do or the way you lead. Position yourself to explore at least once a quarter.

- As you read new information and engage in meaningful conversations, use the Absorb-Convert-Act Model to identify key ways to change and strengthen your leadership development and POV over time. Write it down so the process becomes second-nature.

- As challenges arise and trends develop, use the Absorb-Convert-Act Model to construct better ways to solve new problems and create better solutions with unexpected, positive results.

- Each week, reflect on what you accomplished and how it relates to achieving your larger goals and growing your leadership skills. If you feel your progress is insufficient, drill in to where the converting process is getting hung up. Put practices in place to get unstuck.

WHAT'S NEXT FOR YOU AS ASPEN LEADERS?

Imagine it's 2039. You're no longer the generation that the older ones are looking at. *You* are one of the older generations. What's different?

By many predictions the scenario could be better in part because of your influence. And I'm speaking to "you" not as an individual reader but to "you" collectively—as a generation, as a force, as a dynamic grove of leaders.

Imagine the Millennial Workplace as you have helped create it twenty-five years from now. Employees have more life/work options. They can work from home, from co-working spaces, from rooftops, from cars. Corporations and small businesses have increasing responsibility to make positive social differences and contributions.

Business leaders invest directly in their communities, locally and globally.

That's the far-sighted leadership you bring to the future.

A THIN DIFFERENCE

By coincidence, our stories crossed on that afternoon in the Rockies. I wasn't looking for a guide, but I found one; I wasn't seeking inspiration, but the aspens became a soul spark that has helped me consider anew our generations' mutual leadership abilities.

There are differences in leadership opportunities when I was in my twenties versus now. When I think back on my career path, I wasn't aware of what generation I was in or what that identity potentially meant in the continuum of history. I was a bit short-sighted.

The beauty of your present situation lies in part with the larger digital ecosystem that gives you ready access to knowledge and resources that you can leverage for the better. It's up to you to cut through the noise and focus on what matters most.

Forty-eight, standing among a new generation of leaders just as I stood among that grove of glorious aspens, I am scared and proud. I am scared because I don't want to screw up the future. There's a lot at stake for our mutual future. There are thorny problems that demand our highest leadership potential that transcend our private bank accounts or personal glory. When I hired a talented Millennial for a team position, I actually feared I could not adapt my leadership skills to lift her up effectively enough to keep her onboard. I needed to be open to change and ready to step it up in leadership. I did so. She stayed. We both have grown.

You might be scared, too. There are many issues pressing, and your time is limited. Expectations are high. You will make mistakes, but your intensity of purpose with the help of others can guide you.

I am also proud. I am proud of what Millennials—the generation that my two sons are part of—are bringing to the leadership table, how your story is already having an impact. In my mind and soul, I know you will be the next great generation of leaders, solving leftover problems and taking us to new levels of awareness and unforeseeable purpose-filled results.

It turns out, after all, that there is a thin difference in the alleged "gap" between the generations. We both want the same things: a better, sustainable future.

TAKE THE ASPEN CALL

What's next?

You.

You're next.

Lead the aspen way. Dig deep. Convert your potential. Act beyond your selfish needs. Activate your distinct leadership potential.

This is your time.

GRATITUDE

Raising two teen sons has it rewards and challenges, and they keep me centered, engaged, and always trying to be a better father, person, and leader. I am grateful for my sons and our family generations who built a solid foundation for us to grow upon.

Throughout my career, I have been fortunate to learn from many great people across various generations. Starting as a legislative intern and moving later into a full-time position, United States Senator Jim Abdnor served as a strong character-based role model, demonstrating humility, service, and generosity. My early days in Washington, D.C., served as a solid foundation to stretch myself as well as being trusted to move initiatives and projects forward. To each of the leaders I worked for, thank you for your challenges, guidance, and support, especially Monika Harrison, Richard Doubrava, Bill Dohr, and Paul Bateman.

My business career crossed paths with equally engaging leaders. Bob Swem set the stage by being honest about his leadership transformation and renewed focus on people, process, and quality. His down-to-earth style and mentoring ways delivered great lessons that have stuck with me. Sharon Forman demonstrated how to make partnerships work, and Elizabeth Davis exhibited a steely determination in making an entrepreneurial venture work. William Donahoo radiated energy in all of his work and interactions, connecting people to projects and projects to people. And, finally, Phil Guy who is the person I have worked with the longest. With impeccable character, he truly cares for people and what they want to achieve in life and work. These are some of the wonderful leaders who have developed me through the years at companies like VTEL, QuickArrow, IBM, BMC Software, and Corepoint Health.

As I look forward, I am excited about the generations ahead, especially Millennials. We have interviewed many Millennial leaders, and each story inspires and energizes me. My gratitude to the Millennial leaders who are tackling big and small challenges with purpose and collaboration.

In my writing and publishing efforts, Jeffrey Davis has been a steady, challenging, and guiding voice. I am grateful for his time, insights, and talents. Jeffrey is an amazing and engaging coach. When you are ready to write your story or pursue your creative initiative, call Jeffrey! Tanya Robie has contributed a lot with her editing skills and insights as well. Thank you to the Tracking Wonder team!

Along with Tracking Wonder, the Weaving Influence team helps keep me active and current in various social communities. They deliver intelligent service and support. Thank you, Becky Robinson!

Finally, I want to say a special thanks to Molly Page for her enthusiasm and story writing skills. Molly has done a superb job of capturing many great stories in our Millennial Momentum series on Thin Difference. Molly's social and writing talent is engaging, insightful, and always diligent. She has been a pivotal member of the Thin Difference team. Another source of inspiration is Erica Johansen. Erica brings a contagious optimism to the work she does and in the way she leads. She represents the best of what is ahead.

Thank you for reading *Activate Leadership*. Your time spent here is appreciated more than you will know. I am honored and grateful.

JON MERTZ

Jon Mertz enjoys starting a robust conversation, interacting with thoughtful people, and offering what he can to engage in meaningful actions on how to lead and live in better ways.

A farmer's son, a political appointee during his twenties, and a marketing and business development leader over twenty-one years, Jon has worked in large and entrepreneurial companies like Deloitte, IBM, BMC Software, QuickArrow, and Corepoint Health. In 2014, Trust Across America-Trust Around the World named Jon one of the Top 100 Thought Leaders for Trustworthy Business.

Follow Jon on Twitter @ThinDifference and join the Thin Difference Facebook community. Keep current on the latest insights on Millennial leadership at www.thindifference.com and on Millennial Tempo, a Flipboard magazine.

Printed in the USA
CPSIA information can be obtained
at www.ICGtesting.com
LVHW010801010923
756909LV00004B/598